MW01265583

OUTCAST

OUTCAST

How the Radical Left Tried to Destroy a Young Conservative

GLORIA GIORNO

LIBERTY HILL PUBLISHING

Liberty Hill Publishing
2301 Lucien Way #415
Maitland, FL 32751
407.339.4217
www.libertyhillpublishing.com

© 2023 by Gloria Giorno Group, LLC

Liberty Hill Publishing Elite

All rights reserved solely by the author. The author guarantees all contents are original and do not infringe upon the legal rights of any other person or work. No part of this book may be reproduced in any form without the permission of the author.

Due to the changing nature of the Internet, if there are any web addresses, links, or URLs included in this manuscript, these may have been altered and may no longer be accessible. The views and opinions shared in this book belong solely to the author and do not necessarily reflect those of the publisher. The publisher therefore disclaims responsibility for the views or opinions expressed within the work.

Unless otherwise indicated, Scripture quotations taken from the Holy Bible, New International Version (NIV). Copyright © 1973, 1978, 1984, 2011 by Biblica, Inc.™. Used by permission. All rights reserved.

Paperback ISBN-13: 978-1-66287-972-2

Hard Cover ISBN-13: 978-1-66287-973-9
Ebook ISBN-13: 978-1-66287-974-6

DEDICATION

This book is dedicated to my son, Stevie, and every conservative Christian fighting the good fight. Do not be discouraged. As the Lord says: "Maintain justice and do what is right, for my salvation is close at hand and my righteousness will soon be revealed." (Isaiah 56:1, NIV) Stay true to yourself and the Lord. Kneel to God and stand for the Flag. This book is for those who know right from wrong and are willing to speak the truth. You are the ones chosen to follow the Lord's path. Go make Him proud!

I want to thank my husband, sons and daughter-in-law for their encouragement and support throughout this journey.

Reviews for Outcast

"Outcast: How the Radical Left Tried to Destroy a Young Conservative' is a riveting, thought-provoking exploration of the troubling erosion of free speech and open discourse in our contemporary society. Narrating the harrowing journey of a young patriot navigating the tumultuous seas of higher education, this book shines a disturbing light on the pernicious censorship lurking within our institutions. It serves as a clarion call to all who cherish diversity of thought, pushing us to confront and contest the insidious forces that threaten to undermine the very foundations of our society."

-U.S. Representative Andy Ogles

"Every generation in America should read 'Outcast'. In 2020, the United States was infected with more than coronavirus. A movement of black non-Christian, self-proclaimed victim-activists broke Covid lockdown protocols to garner millions of dollars from fearful and woke sympathizers to ravage cities, influence public policy. And indoctrinate weak organizations. Belmont succumbed to the social justice and racial equity pimps and embraced Black Lives Matter indoctrination over education. The Word of God says, 'The wicked flee when no one pursues, but the righteous are bold as a lion.' (Proverbs 28:1) Gloria Giorno, is as bold as a lion, and her story 'Outcast' explains her righteous stand against the wicked, the liberal left, BLM, and wokeism. 'Outcast' is moving, compelling, and most importantly, a truthful account."

-Linda Lee Tarver, Ed.D., Th.D.

"In an era when so many Americans are despairing of the pervasive wokeness in our universities, one would expect at least 'Conservative Christian' schools would be immune. Not so fast! Gloria Giorno's compelling tale of her son Stevie's devastating sojourn as president of Nashville's Belmont University should serve as a warning of how bad things have become practically everywhere for America's conservative youth. Don't miss this important and enlightening book!"

-Roger L. Simon, award-winning author, Oscar-nominated screenwriter, editor-at-large of The Epoch Times

"Gloria Giorno has exposed what is an enduring example for this generation as conservatives continue to stand with courage in their commitment to God and Country. 'Outcast' tells the

true story that has made Stevie an even stronger and more cou-rageous leader of the Tennessee Young Republicans after the persecution he received at Belmont University in 2020."
-Tamra Farah, National Senior Advisor of FreedomWorks

"Outcast tells us how the higher education system is broken: silencing and discouraging even the strongest of people. It shows what is happening across the nation. 'Outcast' should remind us that we don't need to bend the knee to those who yell the loudest to accomplish what we set out to do- character and truth will always prevail."
-Alexis Wilkins, Country Music Artist

"Outcast is a refreshing and encouraging read for young college students who are constantly inundated with liberal indoctrina-tion. Gloria's story is the epitome of the lengths that the liberal higher education institutions will go to silence anything that goes against the liberal narrative."
-Paige Kuczek, United Women Foundation Contributing Member

FOREWORD

Through this book, its protagonist and author testify to the hope we still harbor for the future of our nation.

Gloria Giorno spent her early childhood years in Communist Yugoslavia, where she witnessed firsthand the dangers of what some would willingly prophesy for the United States of America. Like me, she has seen what our country's "education" system is doing to our young children and the results they've inflicted and continue to impose on our country.

President John Adams assured us, "Our Constitution was meant only for a moral and religious people. It is wholly inadequate to the government of any other."

Our schools began with a movement to ensure Biblical values passed from generation to generation. Over time, nefarious, anti-freedom forces harnessed and perverted this effort. It took time, but with the transition from one-room schoolhouse to assembly-line teaching, division by age instead of ability, and the insistence of academics (the three Rs) replacing full-character instruction, the public's hearts were weaned of the truth and fed the lies of tolerance, and appeasement and the best way forward. Fast forward to the new school system, which despite its earlier objections to doctrine and assurance of academics, now advocates only doctrine and the absence of academics. Proficiency in Ohio is defined as a 38% test score, and Oregon passed a law that high school students need not know how to read or do math for graduation.

Enemies in our school now instruct in moral depravity and an enslaved mentality, evidenced by all the parents who admit to being so uneducated they couldn't possibly teach their young children academics, while insisting on sending their pride and joy into the same system that rendered them inept. It's a form of mental slavery or brainwashing – the refusal to think that was cultivated in our institutions that insist they do the opposite!

For thirteen years or more, young people learn from the "educated" just how necessary that same "educated class" is to their future and the future of their children. Thus, they fasten the shackles, lock them, toss the keys, and enslave generations.

But recent events show a new movement forming – a movement of young people hungry for truth and cognizant of the lies the education establishment has been feeding into the culture for decades. There are young conservative men and women eager to renew the fight for our fundamental way of life, our vital traditions, and essential morals, including truth. They seek to reestablish ranks rooted not in government and corruption, but in liberty and justice for all.

Mrs. Giorno raised one of these valiant young warriors in her son, Stevie Giorno. His story is a cautionary tale and a rousing recounting aimed to inspire. She documents the blinding shift of her son's compatriots from normal college students to angry radicals, the so-called administration class that pursued him, and the complicit, conniving media all within the space of a few months. It highlights the need for parents to reevaluate our very definition of the word "education."

The year 2020 and the Covid mandates and lockdowns – our ill-advised and overreaching responses to an aggrandized threat – exposed the mind-spinning, abusive, anti-child training in our school institutions. Despite the destruction of the pandemic, we can count the revelations of graphic sexual content, Critical Race Theory teachings, false history, and anti-American ideologies forced on our small children to be not simply instructive but motivating. The cry of, "Not on my watch!" has galvanized parents to run for school boards, speak at town hall meetings, and join forces in myriad ways to intervene to protect children from the abusers in the school system.

Unfortunately, many of the harmful fallacies have been ingrained in our children's heads for decades. Today, behold the disastrous results, with lawlessness and atheism on the rise with their correspondent violence. Perhaps more importantly,

OUTCAST

regardless of the proof of abuse in our schools now main-
streamed and obvious to most parents, their own schooling
damaged our current generation of parents to such a degree they
still insist on schooling for their children. Clearly, they give little
thought to what education should be, what schooling is, and
what their hopes and aspirations for their own children might
be. They've succumbed to the "college prep and career readi-
ness" pablum chanted in our institutions and by the teachers'
unions and fail to scrutinize and assess those vague promises.
The brainwashing seems complete. The failure to educate has
rendered the masses incapable of judging their own incom-
petence enough to know they do not know. And so, that cycle
continues.

For a few, though, educating their children through the pandemic response and learning about the horrible standards of
"education" in our schools had the opposite effect. They replied
with, "Even if I fail, it can't possibly be worse than what's happening in the schools." Somehow, these parents analyzed and
weighed the schools' missteps and found them wanting, enough
to pull their kids into the safety of the family unit. This is the
impetus that can save a nation like ours. It is the protective
instinct of the mamma bear and the pappa lion. Those families
are now discovering the beauty and refuge of the home education paradigm. They are freed from the shackles and finding the

joy in relationship and autonomy, away from the clutches of our greedy government and the Machiavellian Marxists.

We must return to the education of our founders – all family-raised, self-taught, or privately tutored, all patriots devoted to freedom to the full extent of their fortunes and honor, all remarkable men. This isn't your mother's homeschooling. It's not Covid-enforced "learning" online. This is biblically guided education of the whole child, with an eye to what the adult will be, not the morbid infantilization that our schools accomplish. It requires the parents to refocus and recommit, be willing to relearn (or learn for the first time) next to (and from) their children, but with it comes tremendous triumphs and rewarding relationships beyond their dreams. It is what God desires for His children. It is, in short, the rebirth of the family unit that undergirded the country and contributed to the greatest leap in prosperity for all that the world has ever witnessed (or likely will again.)

Our children can aspire to greatness when they find security in family, support for their honest pursuits, and freedom in truth – truth that is in the Bible and Godly virtues. Those values and ramparts will empower them to stand up for their beliefs and goals, with national pride and a devotion to serve.

Stevie Giorno embodies those values. The attacks leveled at him were furious and vicious, and yet he stood. His story is a heroic tale of conquering and outwitting evil. We should all prepare our children with such staunch convictions and robust opinions, though we fervently wish they never need them.

As my husband is often quoted, "I had faith, but I never needed faith. Until one day, my faith was tested."

Through home education, we can protect our children from forces that clearly seek their discouragement, damage, and destruction. We can forge strong bonds of family to withstand the fickle cultural shifts and totalitarian inclinations. We can hope our children never be tested, but still imbue them with the backbone to withstand the test that time might bring them.

> For God has not given us a spirit of fear,
> but of power and of love and of a sound mind.
> 2 Tim 1:7

-Sam Sorbo, Author, Podcast and Radio Host, International Public Speaker, and Mentor

CONTENTS

CHAPTER 1: Whatever Happened To Freedom? 1

CHAPTER 2: The Instagram Post That Started It All 11

CHAPTER 3: Abel, Meet Cain 33

CHAPTER 4: Loud and Vengeful. 41

CHAPTER 5: Say it, "Black Lives Matter" 49

CHAPTER 6: Et tu, Brute? 93

CHAPTER 7: Lies, Deceit and Indifference 109

CHAPTER 8: The College Blackshirts 115

CHAPTER 9: Promises Made, Promises Broken 129

CHAPTER 10: The Presidential Debate. 141

CHAPTER 11: The Final Semester. 151

CHAPTER 12: Graduation Day. 157

CHAPTER 13: Afterthoughts As The Battle Goes On 161

I

WHATEVER HAPPENED TO FREEDOM?

Can you imagine a young American being ostracized at a conservative Christian university because he spoke of his love for his country on the Fourth of July?

It sounds like something from a novel about a distant Orwellian future. And yet it happened in the United States, in a part of the country known as the Bible Belt, right here in the 21st century.

It happened to my son, Stevie, a young man who was brought up to love his country, and who has always demonstrated excellent leadership skills. After spending some of my life in a Communist country in Eastern Europe, I have done my best to instill into my children a deep love for the United States and everything it stands for.

And yet, after Stevie openly expressed his love for his country, he was viciously attacked on social media. He was virtually kicked out of the fraternity that had been his "family".

His friends and even his teachers turned against him, calling him a racist and other names.

Surely, this kind of thing can't happen here in the United States, land of the free and home of the brave. It may sound like the worst sort of urban legend. But it's true.

My purpose in writing this book is not to tell my son's story. It goes much deeper than that. I'm sharing what happened to Stevie because I believe it has grave implications for the future of our country and our personal freedoms. Specifically, I believe this is an important lesson for patriotic, conservative Americans. The time has come to stand up for the America we have always known and loved – before we lose her to the forces that seek to destroy her.

We must be vigilant. I believe the radical left is reaching into every area of American life – and especially our schools – using ideologies such as Critical Race Theory to turn our young people against our country. And we are letting it happen. They have disguised their intentions, like the legendary Greeks, who destroyed the people of Troy by presenting them with the "gift" of a giant wooden horse. As you will remember, the horse was full of warriors who charged out of the horse with swords flashing as soon as they were inside Troy's city walls.

If you think I'm exaggerating the situation, I urge you to look at what has happened to higher education in our country. Conservatives are silenced as the radical left is given prominence. Professors are no longer impartial. They are outspoken and looking to brainwash our children. It is almost a totalitarian regime. I am grateful that Stevie lived through the nightmare that we call "higher education."

From the time he was a little boy, Stevie had always loved his country and dreamed of serving her someday. Independence Day was one of his favorite holidays, and, in fact, the whole family joined together in the celebration— enjoying the colorful fireworks, the festivities in the local park, picnics, etc. In this, we weren't much different from the other families in our neighborhood, except that, as I said, the years I spent in a communist country gave me a special appreciation for the freedoms that all Americans enjoy. I had a special love for America that I endeavored to pass on to my two sons.

Stevie was always what I would call patriotic. But he was always good-natured and never judgmental toward others. He was always outgoing and friendly, with friends from a variety of backgrounds and ethnicities. Anyone who would dare to describe him as a "racist" just doesn't know him at all. Although he had strong conservative political views, he never treated those who held different opinions as his enemies. His response, even to those who held the most radical progressive and liberal views was to attempt to win them over by appealing to reason and common sense. He loved to debate and share his views, but he was never one to bully or belittle those who were on the other side of the political fence.

He truly cared about others, seemed to draw them to him, and, because of this was elected to several leadership positions throughout his school years.

In high school, he dreamed of attending college near Nashville. We toured, questioned, and prayed until we thought we had found the "perfect" school. With the help of a conservative Christian professor, we mapped out an accelerated, three-year graduation plan at Belmont University. It was the place that a professor and a friend had recommended for years. With his confidence, I never thought we would come to experience such persecution. No one did. As far as I knew, Stevie had all the willpower to match the means of success provided by Belmont. I was thrilled with his choice.

As time went by, we were more and more convinced that we had made the correct decision. Right from the beginning, Stevie loved school. He made new friends, enjoyed his classes, joined a fraternity, and grew in wisdom and stature. He was no longer a boy, but a man! He was living out his dream and loving every minute of it.

As a part of that dream, he was also deeply involved in the Republican Club on campus and was elected to serve as a Senator in the Student Government Association. In late 2019, he decided to run for Student Government President. He and his Vice-Presidential candidate launched a campaign aimed at improving student/administration communication, engaging more students in student government, instituting recycling on campus and many other initiatives. They ran a great campaign and were elected unanimously.

It should have been no surprise to anyone that Stevie was a conservative Christian Republican. He had been active in Republican politics for years, and that information was prominently posted on his LinkedIn profile and reflected on his Instagram page, both of which have always been public. Since this was a university that purported to be aligned with Stevie's values, we assumed his conservative views resonated well with most students and faculty members.

In January 2020, when COVID-19 was brewing in Wuhan, China, Stevie was sworn in as Belmont University's Student Government Association (SGA) President. He was recognized by the President of Belmont and a room full of guests. The campus administration, and especially his peers, affirmed that there was something special about Stevie.

It's difficult for me to find the words to explain how proud of him I was that day. He seemed so poised, polished, articulate – and handsome. And I wasn't the only one who felt that way. Several of his fellow students told me that they thought the world of Stevie, and that they knew I was proud to be his mother. More than once, I heard, "He's going to do big things someday." It was more than enough to make me stand up a little taller.

The Belmont President also spoke that day and shared about the upcoming 2020 Presidential Debate that would be occurring at the university later that year. In his remarks, he added that Stevie and his Vice-President would have the privilege of being involved with the Debate firsthand and would be an integral part of the student experience.

I want to make it clear that being elected to the office of Student Body President did not change Stevie in any way. He continued to be who he always was, and the students appreciated him for it. Being Student Body President was not a political job and it was important to Stevie to work with students from all walks of life and thoughts. After all, isn't going to college about being exposed to new ideas? Or at least, that's the way it was when I went to college.

My husband and I went home after the ceremony feeling good about what was happening in Stevie's life. He was fulfilling the promise that we had always seen in him, and that made us feel good about the future of our country as well. With young people like our son stepping forward to serve their university, we knew the future of conservatism in the United States was in good hands.

Unfortunately, we were still unaware that a microscopic virus, birthed in a laboratory in China, was about to change everything. COVID-19 was getting ready to unleash its fury on the United States – bringing sickness, death, pitting American against

American, closing schools and businesses, and very nearly destroying the U.S. economy.

Then, in May of 2020, a man's life was taken, and all hell broke loose in America. While every death is a tragedy, what happened following the death of George Floyd in Minneapolis was just as tragic. Our country became divided. The radical left took to the streets across the country and left a path of destruction in their wake. People were killed. Businesses were destroyed. Statues, many of which had been standing strong for centuries, were destroyed. Entire neighborhoods were burned to the ground. Police officers were targeted. Riots were happening on university campuses. America was out of control.

In response to all this turmoil – and especially to the destruction and racial hatred that was taking place on America's university campuses, Stevie, as Student Body President, made a statement on the Student Government Instagram account. The statement called for Belmont students to pray for peace and to remember that SGA will not stand for discrimination of any kind. It also included a reminder that SGA is a family community made up of students serving students:

> *"SGA is dedicated in providing all students on campus*
> *with a feeling of security. We live by "students serving*
> *students" which holds no restrictions. We see our*

community as family and as a family we will continue to fight for justice.

"We were fortunate to have Dr. Maya Angelou on campus in 2011. While on campus she stated, "I agreed to become a rainbow in somebody's cloud who may not look like me. May not share my complexion. May not call God the same name I call God. I agree that I am willing to prepare myself to be a rainbow in somebody's cloud." We urge our students to be the rainbow Dr. Angelou was for so many people. As a student at Belmont, we ask you to never remain silent when you see an injustice, not only on campus, but wherever life takes you. To keep our campus welcoming.

"We are praying for George Floyd's family. We are praying that we see a world where nobody is defined by their race, gender, socioeconomic status, religion, nor sexuality. We are praying for you. We want to ensure that our campus continues to be a safe space for all. SGA has no tolerance for discriminatory acts and will continue to improve campus policy in order to protect all students."

Does this sound like the words of a racist? Stay tuned!

2

THE INSTAGRAM POST THAT STARTED IT ALL

As I've said, the Fourth of July has always been extremely important to our family, which fled from Communist Yugoslavia in 1956 and legally emigrated to the last best hope on earth – the United States. Yugoslavia was considered one of the more "enlightened" of the Soviet satellites. Apparently, there was more "freedom" there. But it wasn't much.

The truth is that people who live in a communist or socialist country are never free.

And 1956 was the year when my parents finally said, "Enough is enough." They fled when they saw the Soviet Union viciously put down a gasp for freedom in another communist country – killing thousands of innocent civilians and driving more than 200,000 from their homes in Hungary. They knew then that there could never be any real freedom in Yugoslavia. Any attempt to change things there would be met with deadly force, just as had occurred in Hungary.

The nightmare there began on October 23, when university students in Budapest rallied at the parliament building to protest Soviet control over their country. When a group of students attempted to enter the government-run radio station to broadcast their 16 demands for economic and political reforms, the police shot and killed several of them.

When word got out about what had happened, thousands of Hungarian civilians took to the streets to join the fight for freedom.

You can imagine how the Soviets reacted. On November 4, Russian tanks rolled into Budapest, surrounding the city. The Hungarian "rebels" put up a good fight that lasted for six days – but they were no match for Soviet power. By the time the fighting ended, some 2,500 Hungarians had been killed, along with 700 Russian soldiers, and 200,000 people had fled from Hungary to seek political asylum in other countries.

My reason for telling you this is not to give you a history lesson, but to illustrate why so many people who have come to the United States from other countries are so passionately in love with this country, and why we are willing to fight to preserve the freedoms we enjoy here. After coming to the United States, my father found work as a diesel truck mechanic before buying real estate in the city of Chicago. My mother was a professor at Loyola University Chicago. As immigrants, my parents knew the horrors of communism and celebrated the freedom to succeed in a capitalist country that valued hard work and character, not skin color or religion. Because of my parents, I have always encouraged my children to celebrate being from the United States of America and to appreciate the opportunities they are given here that they would not have anywhere else.

Stevie was no exception to this. In 2020, our family's 4th of July consisted of doing what just about every family does on the 4th. Watching the hot dog eating contest, sitting at the pool, and eating BBQ. Later that day, Stevie posted a picture I had taken of him standing in front of the White House during a family visit to Washington, D.C. the previous summer.

Liked by billy.mandarino and 342 others

the_stevie_giorno Proud to be an American celebrating the sacrifice of those that gave their all so that we may enjoy the freedom and liberties our forefathers intended on this day in 1776.

His caption with the picture was: *"Proud to be an American celebrating the sacrifice of those that gave their all so that we may enjoy the freedom and liberties our forefathers intended on this day in 1776."* Within the next few hours, his Instagram post exploded. Initial positive comments sharing in the happy occasion were soon drowned out by Belmont's social justice troops marching in to correct the narrative and shame Stevie for being a proud American.

Stevie's crime? Not posting a black square on his Instagram account. Not endorsing "Black Lives Matter" and instead celebrating a "racist holiday." Not complying with the woke mob. One of the most unforgivable sins, Stevie came to learn. His love for America wasn't a good thing, the mob said. Far from it. In fact, it was the ultimate indicator of an evil heart and an evil person. You may be thinking, "There must have been more to it than that," but that is most definitely not the case.

Here are just a few of the comments that came in on Stevie's Instagram that day:

"REMOVE THE RACIST SGA PRESIDENT STEVIE GIORNO."

"Acknowledge the racism surrounding the Fourth of July."

"Racist."

"GKY." (Which I have since learned means, "Go kill yourself.")

And dozens more like these. Within a day, Stevie went from being regarded as a leader beloved by his peers to being considered undeserving of life—simply because he had posted a photograph of himself at the White House and expressed his gratitude for the freedoms that all Americans enjoy! This upcoming generation of leaders spewed hate and vitriol on someone for having a deep and abiding respect for this nation and its founding principles. It became clear that this "conservative Christian university" in Tennessee failed to teach our conservative Christian history correctly. These private school students were direct benefactors of America's blessings of liberty.

And yet, they believe the very day our forefathers stood up against tyranny, the day that brought liberty to themselves, was not a day of freedom but of oppression. It was clear that they didn't understand why they felt this way, because they couldn't even explain the rationale for their anger. They still can't. All they know is that America is an evil country because the mainstream media and their liberal teachers have reinforced that belief their entire lives.

As a mom who considers herself fairly intelligent and educated, I had no idea what they were so angry about. These were well-educated, private school students who had good futures in front of them, talking about how "rich white people" are the root cause of all the evil in the country. Their arguments in the comments section were as confused and erratic as their "activism" in the streets and elsewhere online.

I admit that I was frightened for my son's life. As any caring mother would do, I called the police and asked for their advice. The officer I spoke to urged Stevie to take the threats seriously. He suggested that we report the incident to the proper authorities at the university, and the officer took copies of the social media posts.

Although I feared the worst, I also hoped that it would all blow over and be forgotten. After all, Stevie hadn't done anything wrong. Surely those who were attacking him would move on to other issues, other targets. But that wasn't what happened.

Instead, we discovered that the woke left mob started a change.org petition online, condemning my son for his "racist" views. Several hundred people had already signed the petition. I was livid. These people didn't know my son! They certainly didn't know his heart. I had never heard him say or do anything that had the slightest whiff of racism about it. But his accusers didn't care about that. They had found a new "boogeyman" to persecute, and they were going after him with their knives out. They had used Stevie's campaign slogan "A Better Belmont" with a twist on it and a picture that was my property. You must give them credit for creativity—and just like that, with NO proof, my son became known as a racist.

The headline at top of the change.org petition read, "Remove Stevie Giorno from SGA Presidency." A sub header underneath advised readers that "334 have signed. Let's get to 500!"

It went on to assert that Stevie had posted a "VERY covertly racist post" and that he "refused to acknowledge the racism surrounding the Fourth of July." As someone who loves this country deeply, I had never considered Independence Day to be a racist holiday – and I doubt you had either. When and how did this happen?

Just so you can see for yourself that I am not exaggerating or making any of this up, I am including photos of some of these posts. I have redacted names of the senders and some other information to avoid frivolous lawsuits.

Not only did hundreds of people sign this petition, but there were also many hateful, racist, and untrue comments. I have attached some of them below.

"we need more voices represented than just the rich white population"

The irony that seems to have eluded the author of this post is that she and her family are wealthy and white. In fact, she went to a private high school in Williamson County with Stevie, the wealthiest county in the state of Tennessee. I wondered if her eager involvement to deride her former friend had something to do with how high school ended for her. The causes for people's behavior have always fascinated me.

She had a sour end to her senior year: she wasn't allowed to walk the stage for graduation because she broke school rules and was held accountable. In the years after, her name came up occasionally among our fellow high school parents, always with stories of her acting out against high school friends who she perceived as successful. She was exhibiting, I believe, an ugly trait of the left: jealousy. I meditated on her remark. The harassment against Stevie appeared to be opportune outlets for jealousy.

The rest of the online comments ranged from critical to violent. There were threats of assault and demands for suicide. Through it all, Stevie kept up a stoic front. He received each participant in the online discourse against him with respect and stood firmly by his beliefs. No matter what lies and comments were made, Stevie never took the bait to engage. I thought about how many times I had heard liberal politicians point fingers at conservatives, calling us narrow minded and intolerant. But now their true colors were showing. It seemed clear that the only ones they were tolerant of were those who agreed with them.

But let someone do something they didn't agree with—like celebrating Independence Day—and just watch the death threats fly! It seemed to me that they were about as "tolerant" as the Communist leaders who sent their tanks and soldiers to stamp out the threat of freedom in Hungary in 1956.

The petition even included Stevie's personal Instagram handle, making it easier for those who wished to threaten and insult him.

About a week later, the activist group that created the petition posted a comment expressing their frustration that Stevie still hadn't relented by saying those three words they were craving to read: "Black Lives Matter."

Stevie Giorno STILL Refuses To Acknowledge BLM

It has been a week since this petition began, and the comments on Steve Giorno's Instagram post have QUADRUPLED!

Still, he has not made ANY public statement about BLM....

 Cristina Sayor
2 months ago

"It has been a week since this petition began, and the comments on Stevie Giorno's Instagram post have QUADRUPLED!" bragged the activists. "Still, he has not made ANY public statement about BLM."

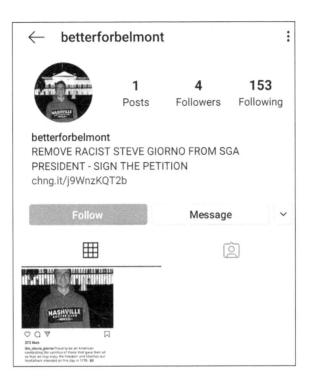

An Instagram page with the username "betterforbelmont." was a screenshot of Stevie's Independence Day post and included the petition in their bio.

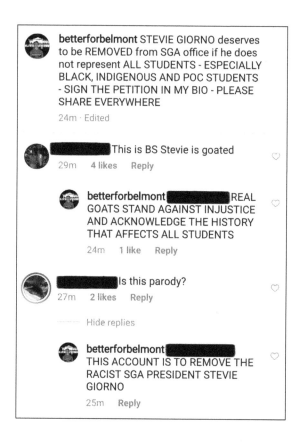

@betterforbelmont: "STEVIE GIORNO deserves to be REMOVED from SGA office if he does not represent ALL STUDENTS–ESPECIALLY BLACK, INDIGENOUS, AND POC STUDENTS–SIGN THE PETITION IN MY BIO."

Some users defended Stevie:

"This is BS Stevie is goated"

@betterforbelmont: REAL GOATS STAND AGAINST INJUSTICE AND ACKNOWLEDGE THE HISTORY THAT AFFECTS ALL STUDENTS"

"Is this parody?"

@betterforbelmont: "THIS ACCOUNT IS TO REMOVE THE RACIST SGA PRESIDENT STEVIE GIORNO"

 betterforbelmont Just to be clear. This page is not meant to bully, but to hold student leadership accountable. If you perceive accountability as bullying, you're part of the problem. That's all.

@betterforBelmont: "Just to be clear. This page is not meant to bully, but to hold student leadership accountable. If you perceive accountability as bullying, you're part of the problem. That's all."

The activists deleted Stevie's picture about a week later. They replaced it with another post and a black square:

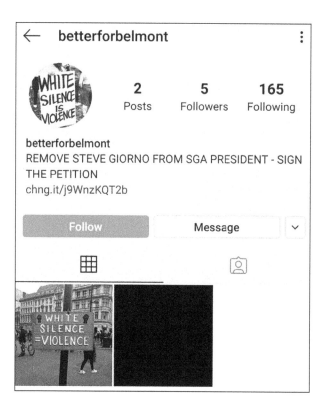

When users criticized their anonymity, the activists claimed that revealing their identities would put them at risk.

betterforbelmont▮▮▮▮▮▮▮▮▮▮ ♡
this account isn't run by one person,
also, obviously you guys are very
very hateful; protecting our identities
isn't "cowardly" if we were bullying
or exposing or pushing for him to
be cancels that's one thing, we are
stating facts, why would we openly
put students of color involved with
this account at risk like that? steve
giorno has NEVER said black lives
matter. this isn't slander that is a
fact. Sorry you don't like it.

@betterforBelmont: "This account isn't run by one person, also, obviously you guys are very very hateful; protecting our identities isn't 'cowardly' if we were bullying or exposing or pushing for him to be canceled that's one thing, we are stating facts, why would we openly put students of color involved with this account at risk like that? steve giorno has NEVER said black lives matter. This isn't slander, which is a fact. Sorry you don't like it."

Following the police officer's instruction, Stevie forwarded all the posts and comments to the proper authority as told to him. The SGA advisor. Of course, this was all with the blind belief that Belmont, an avowed Christian university, would want to protect students under the recommendation of law enforcement. This was not the case. He did nothing. Not even the easiest thing: passing them along to campus police.

Most of the threats were anonymous, but there were a few real names that Stevie recognized. Because I hadn't heard back from Stevie's advisor, I took it upon myself to go higher. This was a small university, so I called the university president's office. I wanted him to assure me that Belmont would do everything possible to assure my son's safety during the upcoming fall semester. An assistant promised me that the president would call me back as soon as possible. I knew she could hear the fear in my voice and told me that the president and his staff were aware of the social action revolving around Stevie.

I had a terrible feeling as I hung up the phone. I felt that I was being patronized, and that no real help was being offered. Anxiety grew within me as time went by and I received no return call. Minutes passed without a phone call. Those minutes became hours, then days. I heard nothing from the school but a deafening silence. Did the president of the university not understand that this was an urgent matter?

I thought back to my sneaking suspicions of Belmont's duplicitous nature during Stevie's freshman orientation in 2018. Words like "conservative" and "Christian" were used often by administrators with a sales pitch self-awareness of Tennessee's red reputation. I wondered then if it wasn't a bill of goods designed to appeal to families like mine and students like Stevie. Very unprofessional, but that seems to be the theme with today's university leaders.

They'll apparently do whatever they need to do to fill their class-rooms and rake in that tuition money.

I recalled the orientation director's smiling face on stage from that day, how he had boasted about the university's "conservative Christian" core. What did he really think? I had no idea where the hatred that inspired over 300 comments came from. These accusations of racism and threats to strip Stevie of all his standing were almost more than I could bear. Still no return call from the president.

Several days went by before I finally got the call I was waiting for. And when it came, it wasn't from the president, but Belmont's lead attorney. I was shocked by the escalation. Why wouldn't the president or someone on his staff return my call? I expected there to be some tension, but the attorney was kind. I discovered that his son was in Stevie's fraternity, and he shared concerns about the political landscape and its bearing on Stevie's presence on campus. He understood my cause for concern. Hundreds of angry or violent comments, a petition, and several new Instagram accounts dedicated to spewing hate at one individual is not exactly something that a parent sees on a regular day with their college kid. His sympathy disarmed me. I let myself believe we were having a civil conversation between two parents, when out of the blue, he asked me.

"Are you going to be suing the school?"

A lawsuit was far from my mind. Stevie's safety was my only concern.

"What would I be suing the school for?" I responded quickly. "I just want to know that my son will be safe on campus, and I want Belmont's assurance of this."

After a few seconds of silence, the attorney promised me that the university would have a plan for Stevie's safety. Of course, it bothered me that it took him so long to say this. But like I said, he seemed like a nice guy, and because he was a parent himself, I felt that he understood how I felt, and that he would see to it that my son was protected. He assured me that someone would reach out to me with the details of that plan.

I'm glad I didn't hold my breath—because it never happened.

What was Stevie supposed to do? Wear a disguise to school? Change his name? Transfer to another school on the other side of the country where the students might not know that Stevie was a repugnant Fourth of July observer? (Yes, I admit that sarcasm has overtaken me here.) The truth was that he wasn't about to back down due to a bunch of people who apparently hate their country, and neither was I.

At that time, rioters from the radical left were turning many of America's cities into warzones. They were torching businesses, fighting police, and attacking innocent civilians. It felt like a purge. Meanwhile, COVID-19 regulations shuttered everyone and everything except those criminals. I saw them in my mind's eye: a fiery, armed, maniacal mob descending upon campus in search of Stevie. His safety preoccupied my thoughts for weeks. Belmont had no intention of helping my son. They had clearly sided with the radical left. Stevie kept reaching out to deans but got no response with one exception. The Student Government Association advisor told Stevie to just ignore the attacks. "They will die down in time," he promised. Famous last words of a fool.

His words reminded me of what I was seeing on television. Prominent news reporters constantly assured the public that the "protests" sparked by the killing of George Floyd were "mostly peaceful". Behind them, smoke billowed up from businesses that had been destroyed by the rioters, many of those businesses black-owned. I felt as if the whole world had gone crazy.

With fires blazing all around him, MSNBC journalist, Ali Velshi said, "I want to be clear how I characterize this. This is mostly a protest, it is not generally speaking unruly, but fires have been started." Miguel Marques of CNN said, "The first thing I want to make perfectly clear is that this has been almost entirely peaceful." Really? He must not have been watching the same riots I was watching.

No wonder I was beginning to have my doubts. Especially when Belmont gave their "endorsement" to Black Lives Matter– a group that in my opinion is violent, fraudulent, and bent on destroying our country. The following is an excerpt of the lengthy email including the endorsement from the university president sent to the entire Belmont community on July 27th, 2020.

> With that said, yes, Black Lives Matter to me and to Belmont. While our country's treatment of Native Americans, minorities and immigrants from all parts of the world has resulted in people being systematically devalued, diminished and destroyed throughout our history, the recently renewed focus on the mistreatment of Black Americans has created a broad outpouring of demands that we bring an end to systemic racism wherever we find it.

"...With that said, yes, Black Lives Matter to me and to Belmont. While our country's treatment of Native Americans, minorities, and immigrants from all parts of the world has resulted in people being systematically devalued, diminished and destroyed throughout our history, the recently renewed focus on the mistreatment of Black Americans has created a broad outpouring of demands that we bring an end to systemic racism wherever we find it."

Only in 2020 would this be the response from a conservative Christian university. It is mind boggling and terrifying to think that the president would think so poorly of a country that has provided more freedom, wealth, and opportunity for all people regardless of race since its inception. Instead, this President saw fit to throw gasoline on the fire and divide students and faculty who did not agree with the tenets of the Black Lives Matter organization. Who in their right mind would want to make things worse and perpetuate the lie that America has been and is an evil, terrible, systemically racist country?

He continued with his unabashed hatred of America by calling for more DEI programs at Belmont.

> Diversity, inclusion, and equity will continue to be embedded in the soon to be announced Vision 2025 plan, but it will also be elevated in our efforts as one of eight broad strategies for the overall guidance of the university.

"Diversity, inclusion, and equity will continue to be embedded in the soon to be announced Vision 2025 plan, but it will also be elevated in our efforts as one of eight broad strategies for the overall guidance of the university."

Ironically, I found that the "DIE" program was named appropriately as it was killing our country. This inspired students to attack other students without remorse and could have been interpreted as permission to go after America loving students.

Still, no one from the university would send a message to students whose names they had and tell them to stop threatening my son. Threats were now acceptable at a conservative Christian university against those who were there to promote the conservative Christian agenda. I was and am still shocked but have learned to expect such a thing in higher education.

3
ABEL, MEET CAIN

J ust in case you're not familiar with the biblical story of Cain and Abel, let me tell you that they were the first two children born into this world – sons of Adam and Eve. Unfortunately, they didn't get along very well. In fact, Cain was so jealous of his younger brother that he murdered him in the world's first case of fratricide—but certainly not its last.

I'm sure that Abel was completely surprised when his brother turned against him, attacking him as they worked in the fields one day. You just don't expect your sibling or siblings to revolt against you.

In Stevie's case, he thought he would find acceptance and sanctuary among the young men who had been his fraternity brothers. No one knew Stevie better than they did. Surely, they had seen that he didn't have a racist bone in his body! And yet, as left-wing activists attempted to impeach Stevie for daring to love America, his fraternity brothers worked to banish him altogether. The instigator was a young man named Kevin, a black man who Stevie considered to be a close friend. After news of the petition to impeach Stevie made its way around the campus, Kevin told the fraternity brothers that while Stevie wasn't racist, his "silence" amounted to "complicity." (Complicity in what?) In fact, Stevie had denounced racism and expressed his commitment to equal and fair treatment of others regardless of race, but Kevin wanted to hear him utter a specific phrase: "Black Lives Matter." He apparently felt that his insight on the matter weighed more heavily than others because he was the only black brother in the fraternity.

He wrote to the other members of the fraternity:

> "I just want to offer my opinion being the sole black person in this fraternity. If you can't say Black Lives Matter in the statement, then the statement is irrelevant. If you are not for the movement, you are against it. And another note on the statement, 'it is our belief that all are created equal by our creator.' Even though we may all be created equal, that doesn't mean we are treated equally in this country. I'm not calling him racist. Much love for Stevie. He is my brother and always will be. My hope is for my brothers to be able to see my perspective in all this."

Kevin and Stevie had been friends who played board games together and hung out outside of fraternity events together. Their fraternity bond made them consider one another brothers. What changed? Racism was never a barrier between them. That was, until Kevin decided it was. Things only got worse. Nothing Stevie said would dissuade him from bending Stevie to his will.

Stevie didn't recognize this at first. He saw a hurting friend, so he messaged his fraternity brother privately to remedy the situation. Kevin thanked Stevie for reaching out. He acknowledged, again, that Stevie was not racist. He assured Stevie that he loved and supported him. Their online conversation went as follows:

> **Kevin:** *"Thank you for reaching out Stevie! It means a lot. I want you to know I wasn't attacking you and I know you are not racist. I acknowledge your hard work behind the scenes and appreciate it. I just wanted to offer a poc [person of color] point of view in the group chat because someone brought up the topic and wanted to just explain how people were feeling and where they were coming from. I love and support you as your brother and friend!"*

> **Stevie:** *"I appreciate you looking out for me. The VP and I have done our best to make sure everyone knows*

our door is open. I'm sad that people haven't said anything to us before this post about how they were feeling. I don't want people to fight with one another."

Kevin: "Yeah I know it has probably been overwhelming receiving all of this feedback, but I believe people are coming from a good place and just want to see change happen in this world and on campus with everything going on in the world right now. It's good to hear you and the VP are working hard and will take these concerns and hopefully push them forward on the university campus for change."

With that, Stevie "liked" Kevin's message. He didn't feel the need to respond further because he thought they'd reached an amicable end to the conversation. But Kevin followed up an hour later. It wasn't enough for him to respect their differences. No, that couldn't be the end of it. Stevie *had* to say, "Black Lives Matter."

Kevin: "I just want to add one more thing that was a big issue for a lot of people. It is important when making a statement that it specifically says 'Black Lives Matter', or it won't be received correctly and that was a big issue for a lot of people in the comments.

Once again much love but just want to expand and
speak on the issue that many people were upset over."

That seemed like the end of it. A month passed and nothing else was said. Stevie would not be bullied into making a statement. He is a Christian and BLM is not remotely close to having any Christian values. Does Stevie believe that the lives of black people are as precious as the lives of white people, or brown people, or any other color of people? Of course, he does. But he cannot support the organization Black Lives Matter, because some of their beliefs are anti-American and anti-Christian.

For example, Black Lives Matter's founders are dedicated Marxists, they oppose the Christian view of marriage, destroy the nuclear family, and disparage capitalism, which they call – what else? – "racist."

Incidentally, I am not the only one who feels this way about the Black Lives Matter organization. Here is a small sampling of what some other "respectable" voices have said about them:

"The stated goals of Black Lives Matter are anti-Christian." —Decision Magazine, July 1, 2020.

"Black Lives Matter continues to harm America." —The Heritage Foundation, February 7, 2022.

"Poll: 57 percent have negative view of Black Lives Matter." —The Hill, August 2, 2017.

"BLM has left black Americans worse off since the movement began." —Fox News, May 12, 2022.

This is just a small sample, showing that many Americans are not fans of the Black Lives Matter movement. I know that many evangelical Christians support Black Lives Matter, but I can't understand how that is possible, when the organization's official policy says things like the following:

"We affirm the lives of Black queer and trans folks, disabled folks, undocumented folks, folks with records, women, and all Black lives along the gender spectrum. Our network centers those who have been marginalized within Black liberation movements.

We are guided by the fact that all Black Lives Matter, regardless of actual or perceived sexual identity, gender identity, gender expression, economic status, ability, disability, religious beliefs or disbeliefs, immigration status, or location. We make space for transgender brothers and sisters to participate and lead. We are self-reflexive and do the work required to dismantle cisgender privilege and uplift Black trans folk, especially Black trans women who continue to be disproportionately impacted by trans-antagonistic violence.

We disrupt the Western-prescribed nuclear family structure requirement by supporting each other as extended families and 'villages' that collectively care for one another, especially our children, to the degree that mothers, parents, and children are comfortable."

Yes, it is wrong to discriminate against someone based on their skin color, ethnicity, or any other such reason. But Black Lives Matter seems determined to make things worse, rather than better.

4

LOUD AND VENGEFUL

Kevin messaged again in August, right before the semester began. Gone was the amicable tone from his previous messages. This time, his tone was more menacing. Kevin told Stevie that he would be loud and vengeful. With that, Kevin joined the ranks of other students at this so-called conservative, Christian university threatening Stevie.

> *Kevin: "Hi Stevie. I've realized you have not replied to my previous message and have kept silent on a response. So, if you say you are my friend/brother and care for me and my well-being, as well as the entire student body, why have you still not said Black Lives Matter? I want you to know that I will not stay silent and quiet until I hear from you. I will continue to seek [you] out until justice is made. There is a rumor going around as to what your stance is on the movement*

and you're reasoning to stay silent. Someone you have worked closely with has confirmed this. My hope was for this not to be true because I have believed you, and what you have told me you stand for and believe in and what you hope to accomplish as SGA president, but I fear at this point that is ignorant for me to believe."

Based on Kevin's remarks, I suspected he wasn't the only student with this mindset. His threat and the unknown masses plotting against Stevie kept me up for nights on end. That threat—*I will seek you out until justice is made*—prompted Stevie to file a police report. The officer advised Stevie to not engage with Kevin after that, and Stevie didn't. He couldn't, really, since shortly after that interaction he contracted COVID-19. But Kevin wasn't done.

Two nights later at 10 pm, Stevie got a call. It was Nathan, the fraternity's risk management chair, who was also his big brother in the fraternity. Normally, physical safety and well-being are the concerns of this leadership role: things like legal and safe alcohol consumption, transportation to events, and hazing prevention. As it seemed to be for everything else in the world that year, all norms, and expectations were tossed out the window.

Nathan told Stevie that if he didn't publish an Instagram post where he would apologize for being proud to be an American and include the phrase, "Black Lives Matter," then the fraternity would come after him.

"[People in this fraternity will do] whatever it takes to destroy your reputation at Belmont and in your future," he said.

If Stevie didn't fall in line with the ideological march of this woke infantry, the person responsible for guaranteeing their safety and well-being couldn't — wouldn't — guarantee Stevie the same rights.

The line had been crossed. Stevie knew he could no longer rely on goodwill from his brotherhood. He arranged a Zoom meeting with Belmont's campus security and included me on the call. He once again provided every single text, email, etc. for campus police to review. I repeatedly voiced my concern for my son's safety, but this didn't seem to be of any interest to them. They kept dismissing the threats as freedom of speech.

Okay, I'd say—what about Stevie's freedom of speech? What if the students who were bullying and threatening him decided to act? No, no—they're excused because they're emotionally aggrieved by a stranger's death. Therefore, Stevie and all the rest of us must accommodate them with a speech they approve of. After all, liberals lose their minds over free speech that does not agree with what they have been brainwashed to say. Belmont was clearly never concerned with my son's safety.

The only options for ensuring Stevie's safety made it more obvious that he had a target on his back. For example, he would not be allowed to bring his car onto campus. Instead, he would have to be driven by a friend and call security upon his arrival on campus. Security would then intercept him and escort him to class. I wondered at their response. My son was penalized after honoring our country on his own Instagram page, while these radical leftists threatening violence were given no such orders. I remembered distinctly their freshman orientation speeches on zero tolerance for bullying and threats. They may as well have set fire to the school handbook.

Only one officer seemed to understand my concerns. He indicated that this silencing of Stevie's concerns was wrong, but he was overridden by the administration.

Why was my son the one forced to bear the brunt of all this? The only reason I could see is that he is a conservative Christian. They wouldn't have to worry about him retaliating with violence. It was easier to prevent Stevie from provoking the beast further. It was decided that nothing would be done with our evidence of students making threats to Stevie. Absolutely nothing. Stevie was on his own on campus except for the one officer escort. He was not allowed to have SGA meetings, be on campus for lunch, just be a normal student. Nope. My son was being punished for being a Christian conservative.

That same day, Stevie met with two deans on Zoom. The pair advised Stevie to ignore the upset masses entirely. Stevie suggested emailing the student body to explain that racism and discrimination are wrong, but the pair told him that it would do more harm than good and that he should not say anything. It was interesting, however, that Belmont's president sent a similar email saying that racism and discrimination were wrong, yet the Student Body President was not allowed to make such a claim. Stevie was being silenced but why? What was Belmont afraid of?

While his enemies could speak, protest, and threaten however they saw fit, Stevie was prevented from reaching out to the students who elected him and making his position on the matter clear.

I found this rather cowardly behavior strange for a university that proclaims, "We are a Christ-centered, student-focused community, developing diverse leaders of purpose, character, wisdom and transformational mindset, eager and equipped to make the world a better place." But how can you develop leaders of diverse purposes and character when you're afraid to rock the boat? How can you say that your values are integrity, inquiry, collaboration, service, and humility when you are afraid of dialogue?

As he dealt with COVID-19, new security protocols, and lack of support from leadership, Stevie responded to Kevin sporadically. It seemed to bother Kevin that death threats took precedence over perceived racism. He would message Stevie until he received a response:

Stevie: "Hey Kevin. I was recently exposed to someone with COVID and I have been out of it for some time and need to quarantine. I think of you as a friend and you know my character and that I am against racism and discrimination of all kinds. I am working on some projects and partnerships for Belmont to make positive changes. When I'm well, I'd like to meet with you and hear your suggestions. Would you be willing to meet?"

Kevin: "Based on your social media and how you have chosen to present yourself it's not obvious you are against racism. It's honestly insulting. You have also chosen to ignore my last couple of messages which I feel also speak to your character. You have heard my concerns so I just want to know how meeting in person will change that? Silence is complicit."

A few hours later, Kevin continued to message.

Kevin: "You have proven my point exactly."

Kevin: "So are you just refusing to respond?"

At this point, Stevie had caught wind that the animosity toward him had shifted from Kevin to his other brothers. Stevie heard rumored threats of blackmail, and even assault. So, he finally responded, again attempting to make peace — but still he refused to give Kevin what he wanted.

Stevie: "*Kevin, I am not refusing to respond. I had to move out of my house because I had Coronavirus and my mom had oral surgery. I just moved back into my house because we had to quarantine separately. I hope you know that I value our friendship and you're entitled to your opinion. Please know that I respect you and I want to continue to be your friend. We may not agree on everything and that's ok because we live in America and we can agree to disagree and still be friends. If you want my thoughts on what you're referring to, I've posted numerous times that I am against racism and discrimination. That being said, I hope you and your orientation group are doing well and I hope to see you all on campus soon.*"

Kevin couldn't agree to disagree on the Black Lives Matter organization. He clearly didn't believe that Stevie was against racism and discrimination. He took it upon himself to escalate the situation to a higher authority that could possibly force Stevie to do his bidding: the Fraternity Standards Board.

5

SAY IT: "BLACK LIVES MATTER"

With Belmont refusing to do anything but make it clearer that Stevie was on his own, the woke infantry closed in further on him. They were considerate about their advance, at least. They gave Stevie four days to get settled in his new classes.

Then on Sunday, August 23rd, Stevie received an email from Nathan, informing him that Kevin had referred him to their Standards Board, and that a meeting would be held to discuss my son's behavior. He didn't put it this way, of course, but it seemed that Stevie was on trial, and that his future at Belmont was at stake.

What exactly had he done to warrant such persecution? He had expressed his love for his country without somehow managing to bring Black Lives Matter into his remarks.

A meeting of the Standards Board would normally be reserved for members who'd broken fraternity rules or the law. Seeing as Stevie had done neither, I had an immediate foreboding sense that this meeting had a predetermined outcome. I felt certain that this meeting would be about as fair as it was for Christ when He went before the Sanhedrin. And I pretty much got it right.

Nathan's email informed Stevie that the Board would set up a meeting via Zoom to "settle things" between the two brothers. They assured Stevie specifically that he would not be verbally attacked, and that both brothers would receive equal speaking time. With these promises, Stevie agreed to this meeting. The meeting was scheduled for that Thursday.

The best way I know of to explain what happened that day is to present the transcripts, as I have done earlier. Before we get into them, I want to acknowledge that spoken conversations are generally not as articulate as written ones. In a verbal conversation, we may repeat words, stammer, or use colloquialisms or other common expressions we wouldn't use in a written paper.

I have made only a few edits to what follows, primarily only to eliminate excessive repetition or to add clarity. I have made every effort to be fair and to protect the dignity of all the young men involved.

On August 26, the day before the meeting, the Standards Board asked to talk to Stevie. Their conversation went like this:

> *Nathan: "I feel like you maybe know kind of what's going on. You were essentially referred, and we know*

that you've had some trouble relating certain views or whatever with Kevin and essentially this has gotten to us in some sense and basically, we just kind of feel like we need to get a conversation going. it's not a situation where we're like 'here's a punishment,' or something. It's not like anything you've necessarily done that the fraternity has any place to do anything about, you know what I mean?"

Mark: *"Basically what we discussed is we need to have a conversation, the six of us with Nathan being the fourth or the fifth [to join], I guess, and then Kevin being sixth. We just need to have you guys sit down and we're going to facilitate a conversation between you two. We just kind of feel like both of y'all...your needs aren't being met properly...We just want to sit down, the six of us, and discuss this and make sure everyone's voiced an opinion in a live sense, more so than over text because a lot can get lost in translation over text. We want to facilitate this just to achieve some sort of resolution for this moment, this kind of issue we have here. And again, we're not punishing you or him. Nobody's wrong right now. Because this has come to us on Standards, we just have decided that the best bet to pursue this and have everyone happy* *or semi-happy is to do a six-person meeting where Standards will facilitate it and everyone's talking it out and everyone's...had a seat at the table and we're done. Does that make sense?"*

Nathan: *"That's kind of where we landed. Do you have any thoughts on that?"*

Stevie: *"Well, you know, I just kind of think the whole thing's unfortunate. the whole texting thing. The last couple of weeks, I've had the Coronavirus. Just going through that alone [was] pretty tough, and especially hearing the stuff that was told to me of what the other brothers have been saying: threatening me, black-mailing me, whatever you want to call it, it's inappro-priate. I'm not a bad person. I always try to be the best person I can be, and that includes listening to people. I won't always see eye-to-eye with everyone, but I think there should be some sort of respect there. I've tried to be respectful with everything I've done and everything Student Government is doing. I feel like a big issue with this is that people just aren't looking into it all the way. If people looked into it, they would see I've been very clear that I'm against racism and discrimi-nation. At the end of the day, that's what this is about:*

someone is accusing me of being racist and that's not true. And in fact, one of the people who accused me of that sent me a text which was the complete opposite, in which he said, 'I know you are not racist. Much love, you are my brother.' It's just very upsetting because I was told that they're going to try to do whatever it takes to destroy my career, my future, when I've done nothing wrong, and I've worked my entire life to build a good reputation. I've done nothing wrong. I've made it very clear; I will not be forced to endorse an organization that goes against my religious principles. I can't do it. Nathan did call me [the day I got Coronavirus] and he told me everything. I said I had to talk to my parents and my pastor, [but] I just can't get behind an organization that calls for the destruction of statues of Jesus Christ."

Logan: "Totally understand all of that. It's very unfortunate that you've been accused falsely of these things and that people have been slandering your name. You know, tensions are high right now for everyone everywhere. I think this conversation, it'll be hard for all of us to have. You'll voice your thoughts and opinions for sure, and Kevin will voice his. Basically, from the sound of things, he just needs to get stuff off his chest *and say stuff. Might not necessarily be true and might just be that he's getting more and more ramped up as time goes on here and he just kind of needs to word-vomit this to all of us and just be like, 'Look, listen, and just don't bother.' And then you, in turn, can listen and you guys can have this discussion. I think that's going to be a lot more helpful right now than messaging. I think he more than likely doesn't mean a lot of this stuff, and anyone else who's falsely accusing you of all this is not digging deeper, doing their homework. I agree with a lot of what you just said, but I think this dialogue needs to happen...We just have to get it all out on the table."*

Stevie: *"Well, you know, I think I understand that but I'm a human being, too, and I shouldn't be subjected to abuse: verbal or anything to do with my career or anything like that. I should not be harassed by a brother of our fraternity. That's what it is. I'm being harassed. It's getting to a point now where it is affecting me and I'm getting very upset about it, because I've tried being the bigger person. I've tried to communicate with him and tell him that I am not racist—just like he said in the message—but you know, I will not be treated poorly. I deserve to be treated like a human being and like I'm* *a brother in this fraternity. A lot of people have been saying, including Kevin, that we aren't doing anything. We haven't announced it yet, but just because we haven't announced it yet doesn't mean we aren't taking action. Things take time. I'm fine talking to him, but I will not be harassed. I will not stand for that. That's not what we should do as brothers. At the end of the day, I hadn't done anything wrong. I'm more than happy to listen to him, but I will not be treated poorly. We're brothers: we deserve to be treated equally and fairly. I just do not feel like that's happening at all. People are allowed their opinions, but when it turns to a point of harassment or defamation or slander or libel, which is when it becomes an issue."*

Mark: *"I completely agree with you. Certainly, we're not going to allow him to just sit there and yell at you or accuse you of things. The idea is that, hopefully, this will put an end to any harassment that's going on. I think fundamentally y'all disagree on some stuff, but at least we can hopefully reach some sort of compromise and an end to the current tension that's happening."*

Logan: *"I think it's very important to know that we're not out to get anybody. We're just trying to mend a* relationship...I can't say I understand what you're going through, but you're heard here. This is a safe place here. We're not going to let you get steamrolled, [or let] him be steamrolled. We just wanted you guys to have a conversation [in] the hopes that something beneficial can come from it."

Mark: "I think the next steps for us will be just to set up a meeting that everyone can attend...But if you have any more questions feel free to ask us those now."

Stevie: "I just want to thank you guys. I know the stuff going on with George Floyd, with Breonna Taylor, I know it's causing a lot of people to be hurt, [and] a lot of tension. I know the coronavirus is definitely having a big effect on that. In normal times, I think we could've resolved this differently and with less stress, but it is what it is, and we have to try to make the best of it. I just appreciate you guys doing your research and trying to find out that I've tried to be a good person and that everyone in the fraternity tries to be a good person. I just wanted to thank you for, you know, not punishing me for something I didn't do. If I can think of any questions, I'll let you know. I want this to be over. I hope you guys never have to worry if someone's going to come after you, whether it's physically [or emotion-ally]. Not only does it bother me, but obviously I don't want to put my parents at risk or anyone I work for. That's always the reason, once stuff like this happens, I try to make sense of it, [and] I try to put it to bed. I didn't do anything wrong."

Logan: "Yeah that's what we're hoping to have with this conversation here is just to get this over quickly and reach some level of resolution between everyone involved here enough that it's satisfactory. Whether or not it's perfect, we don't know, but at least satisfac-tory enough that this stops for you, this stops for him, nobody's looking over their shoulder, no reputation is on the line. We're all back to as normal of a reputation as anyone can have despite all that's been going on..."

Stevie: "It's just unfortunate. I don't want to say it again. It's very mentally [straining with the pan-demic] — we have school that's never been done like this before, a job that's not been done like this before. I'm not a victim, so I don't want you to think that. It's a lot to go through."

Nathan: "*It's okay to be in a bad place. I'm here for you. We all love and respect and care for you so much.*"

With that, the meeting concluded. Stevie felt good about what had been said. Unfortunately, the promises made to him were not truthful and Stevie had been given a false sense of security. When the actual meeting began on August 27, the attitude was far different than what he had been told to expect. Once again, the best way I can share this with you is by giving transcripts of what took place that day. Obviously, what I've included here does not include everything, but I've tried to include all the pertinent details.

Nathan: "*We're excited to have you guys here. We've discussed, everyone here at standards, what's been going on. We figured that this was going to be the most effective way to reach a solution for everybody. We want to make some points about where you all stand, and I hope everybody can reach an agreement about what needs to be done. We want to set some ground rules. This is meant to be a very respectful conversation. We want this to be super uplifting. We want to be encouraging to everybody. We do have the power to mute everybody, so if things start to amp up and get out of hand — not that that will happen because you both are very respectful men, and this is going to be an awesome conversation — but we will use it if we need to. We hope that this is the only conversation we have to have, and everyone can go home feeling good about this. It's clear to me that you both are fighting on the same team, but you have conflicting ways of going about the solution. We are just wanting to lay out a few points."*

"Stevie, Kevin has made it clear to you and to me and to all of us where he stands. He's spoken to a lot of black members of Belmont's community, a lot of alumni members of the fraternity, and of course a lot of alumni members of Belmont, and they all feel, including Kevin, that what SGA stated about Black Lives Matter, specifically in SGA's post about it...has made people on campus uncomfortable and it has made people on campus feel like they don't actually have the support of SGA despite what has been said. What Kevin has made clear is that what he would like to see is SGA and you specifically to make a statement saying that you do stand with the black students of Belmont, you recognize Black Lives Matter, and that you...want people to feel welcomed and comfortable on campus. Kevin obviously felt like that wasn't the case. Kevin felt like

you weren't embodying what being a fraternity man was by not making that clear. He saw what he felt were incongruencies between what you said and what was actually happening."

"That's why we received the referral and that's why we're here today. Kevin, from what we understand as far as hesitations from Stevie are that he doesn't want to connect with Black Lives Matter as a political organization so that's been a clear point made. From what I understand, [Kevin,] what you said is that you don't believe Black Lives Matter is a political statement at all; this is purely a human rights issue for you?"

Kevin: "Correct, no, it's not a political statement."

Mark: "Right. So that would be something we would need to make clear. We read the conversation you guys had over GroupMe. It seemed that Stevie was having a tough time. Kevin, you felt like he wasn't being proactive enough in responding to you about your points and I think that what happened was there wasn't enough being said and points weren't made clear enough, not on your part but specifically on Stevie's part with his responses. You felt like you were offended when Stevie *was [asking to] agree to disagree and still be friends. What Stevie I think was really trying to say was he feels like he's been vocal enough about his stance on equality and human rights and he shouldn't have to justify that. Is that where you're coming from Stevie? Because that's apparent to us."*

Stevie: *"Well, yes, I think I've been very clear that I think racism and discrimination are wrong."*

Mark: *"Yeah; so, you know, obviously there's a big group of people at the university who don't feel that way. With all that being said, we Standards have a solution we are comfortable with but what we want is to let you guys talk with all these points that have been said. I would just like to see if you guys, between the two of you, can reach a comfortable solution."*

Kevin: *"Yes. On that note, I actually did come with some notes written down."*

Mark: *"In the interest of brevity, if we could be as to the point as possible..."*

Kevin: *"I'll read it verbatim. Okay, let's start with your Instagram post, Stevie. It was captioned, 'Proud to be an American celebrating the sacrifice of those that gave their all so that we may enjoy the freedom and liberties our forefathers intended on this day in 1776.'"*

"If you don't understand why this is problematic, let me explain it to you really quickly. How many of those [Founding] Fathers do you think owned slaves and how many of them intended freedoms and liberties for the black people of this country? This post was extremely tone-and time-deaf and honestly insulting. You know what, you're allowed to have your own political views. I can 100 percent respect you if you are different in your outlook on foreign policy and taxation, but black lives are not a political issue. It became personal when you posted that on social media because it was obvious this was not a political conversation. Stevie, I know you're not stupid. You know exactly what you were doing when you posted something like this. You knew how people would react and for you to message me and say the good thing about living in America, [is that] we can agree to disagree and still be friends? Here's the thing: not on human rights we won't. Not if my life matters or not. And then on top of that, for you to post

a picture a few weeks later captioning, 'uncancellable,' while there was still controversy on your last post?"

"I mean you acknowledged there was a problem. And you were okay with it. You just didn't care. So, Stevie, let me ask you one more time: how are you against racism and discrimination of all kinds? Because if what you told me a few weeks ago is true when we were private messaging, what actions have you taken and are you taking? Because it seems you can't take the smallest and most simple action of all which just starts with saying the three words: Black Lives Matter."

Mark: *"Thank you, Kevin."*

Stevie: *"Well first, I had no intention of getting people upset. What it was, was a post thanking those who have died in the line of duty, whether they served in the military or the people who came before us so we would have the opportunity to have this conversation we're having today. In many places we're not allowed to dis-agree: it's whatever someone says we have to agree on. So, you know, there was never any malice towards anyone in it. What it was, was thanking those people before us who gave us the opportunity to do what we* *do today, which is to disagree, and that's okay. You had mentioned the 'agree to disagree' thing that I said. I value your life, we've played Board games together, we've hung out together. I value your opinion, you as a person, and we've always gotten along. It's unfortunate that in the past couple of weeks that's deteriorated, because I consider you a friend, I still do."*

"You had asked what we are doing in SGA to show we're against racism? Well, we've had a lot of meetings, we've reached out to some members of [the Black Students Association], and we haven't released this yet because we haven't finalized it yet, but we're going to be having speakers in a few weeks when we have one of our first meetings. Secondly, we're going to be having minority student liaisons and they're going to be having a role in ensuring SGA hears the concerns of students."

"And lastly, to your point of BLM: I disagree with the organization, and your life is important to me and the lives of every student at Belmont matters to me, especially those who have felt bullied or prejudiced against or had any wrongs against them. I want to make it

clear that I am with you, and I am not against you. I am just against the political organization."

Kevin: "Okay, I'm just going to touch base on every-thing you said. So even though your post wasn't meant to cause an uproar, it obviously set one that's lasted in the community. As the president of SGA, I think it's your duty to address that. I think that was poor plan-ning on your part, that you would not see the correla-tion between those things and then [have] silence on people's feedback on it. I keep touching back to this: you saying, 'Black Lives Matter' has nothing to do with politics. It has nothing to do with if you agree that these monuments need to be torn down, or if you agree with the protests and the looting."

"It angers me when people try to find things that the Black Lives Matter movement is connected to, to call it a political stance or just to be like, 'That's why I can't say it.' Black people are dying daily from police brutality. This system is fucked up. The thing is, as SGA president, of course we feel like you should be speaking on behalf of the entire student body. Black people, white people, minorities all over this campus

are reaching out to you, asking, 'Please Stevie, just say, "Black Lives Matter."'

"We don't feel welcomed and appreciated on this campus. In this political climate, all we want you to say is 'Black Lives Matter,' and if your only argument is like, 'Look, I don't agree with the political stance'—there is no political stance. The three words [are] simply just acknowledging that Black Lives Matter in this country and that you don't agree with systematic racism. No one is going to connect any other thing than that when you're saying it. I don't get that argument at all. It just seems like you're digging for reasons why not to say it. It's just really upsetting because you can't agree to disagree on that. You cannot say you are [against] racism and discrimination and [not] acknowledge that Black Lives Matter. I'm not asking you to donate $100, Stevie, to Black Lives Matter and show the receipts of you doing it. No one's asking you to do that. No one's asking you to go to downtown Nashville and protest or walk hand-in-hand with these people. No one's asking that. We're asking for the bare minimum here...And I guarantee you as we're getting closer and closer to getting back on campus [after COVID] more people are going to speak out and use their voices. This is

ridiculous, that I'm having to sit here on this call. You went on social media and embarrassed this [fraternity]. We released two 'Black Lives Matter' statements highlighting what we're doing as an organization to make sure that we fight against racism and discrimination on this campus, and we want people to know that we stand with these black people, that we stand hand-in-hand and that we acknowledge that Black Lives Matter."

"Here we have an active member, and you, as president of SGA, you are held to a higher standard. You are on a platform where every move and action you do not only reflects on the university but also, you guessed it, the fraternity. It's just embarrassing, the amount of associates that reached out to me, even [those] that dropped, that were like you know, Kevin, I wanted to be part of this organization, but it seems that Stevie and some of the other people's actions — specifically your actions on Black Lives Matter, I just can't associate anymore. As the sole black man of this fraternity, what am I supposed to say? How do I look sitting back letting this happen? I'm over here having to fight with not only you right now but the entire organization to get these things across. At the end of the day,

no offense to anybody, but you don't understand the amount of things black people have to go through right now. I can't even leave my house at night and feel safe. Which is not what this conversation is about. I'm not going to veer off into a different subject. I'm just going to leave with that, Stevie. I kind of foreshadowed this happening. I was like, you know at the end of the day Stevie's not going to say, 'Black Lives Matter.' He's not going to acknowledge this happening. It's just really really upsetting."

Nathan: "If I could interject right there? What I'm hearing from Kevin is that it's not you [want] Stevie just to acknowledge it. [Stevie,] you had a great list of action items that SGA is doing with the liaisons, between the minority student associations and helping to make people feel more welcome and included on Belmont's campus, but I think where the disconnect is happening is Kevin is saying you need to be more vocal about it and there needs to be a louder conversation happening and there needs to be louder support from SGA. It's great SGA has these action items that are happening, and I know that it's not finalized so you haven't announced it yet. But I think I would love to hear what you think about this. I think it's probably

*Stevie's turn to respond. And, Kevin, I'm looking for-
ward to your response. Is something where you [can]
consult with Kevin and some other black members of
the university's community and maybe craft something that discusses again explicitly where SGA stands
and then also says, 'Hey we've got things that are in
the works that are happening!' I don't know how soon
you're planning on releasing those but perhaps you
could make one big statement where, you know, we
would like to just be a louder voice. I think that's all
Kevin is saying. And, of course, that Black Lives Matter.
That here is where the main point is. That's gotta be
clear. And the only way that's going to be clear is if
it's explicitly stated. And I think that's what needs to
happen is just there needs to be a louder voice. With
that, Stevie, whenever you're ready."*

Stevie: *"I just want to say that I've always tried to
make everyone feel included. It makes me very sad
to hear that there are many students who don't [feel
that way]. We'd love to have them come to speak at a
meeting: they're going to be open on Zoom, so we'd love
to hear from students. I disagree with you, Kevin, and
I think that it's—I just don't understand how there's
a difference between the organization [and a political*

statement]. I'm just hung up on that, you know, cause your life is important to me. Everyone on Belmont's campus. I'm trying to do what is best for everyone. But I disagree with the organization and the organization has co-opted the statement. The statement is correct, yes, it is true, but I cannot get behind an organization that goes against my faith and calls for the destruction of the nuclear family. The leaders have called for the destruction of statues of Jesus Christ. I've talked to my pastor about this, I just can't get over that. I can't get over it."

Kevin: "Wow. You know, I made that point. The fact that you can't say 'Black Lives Matter'— I'm not even going to further the conversation on that because we're going to go back and forth all day. By you saying that and letting everybody else on this call know Stevie that's how we see your character. That's how we see your thoughts on racism and discrimination. And you know what? Hold on, I had another note here."

Nathan: "Stevie, Kevin has already stated that he's not even for any of the violence or anything that the actual political organization that it's morphed into — any of that. He's not for that. It's not even about that *for Kevin. This is purely human rights. Obviously, I think it's clear. We've agreed [that] what we're calling for is that there has to be a statement made, and if in that statement — if it helps when you're working with Kevin and other black members of the community to craft a statement — I don't think anybody's going to have any problem with you denouncing any violence or anything that has come out of Black Lives Matter movement. All you're saying is exactly what you already believe, which is that Black Lives Matter and that you stand with that, which you've stated on this call."*

Mark: *"You just have to put it into words and physically write it down on a statement and put it out there."*

Kevin: *"Exactly."*

Mark: *"Nobody's going to turn around and go, 'Well hold on, this guy believes all this political stuff.' It's the human rights issue. We just need Stevie and SGA to literally say 'Black Lives Matter' and basically verbatim what Kevin told us on this call. Just write that down. That's gonna help a lot and people are gonna be a lot more on board. You're not gonna lose followers.*

It's just the statement that has to be made for everyone to be more so on board than where we're at."

Kevin: "No one was going to make that connection. And honestly, do you use your Christianity as a cop-out to not say the statement? Like, I'm sorry I'm just going to be up-front: that was ignorant as hell. And the thing about it: honestly, if that's how you feel and you don't stand for Black Lives Matter, step up and say it. Let people know. Don't hide behind it and try to mask [with], 'Oh oh! If we don't say it and we don't ever address it no one will ever know.' No, if that's how you believe [then publicize it] just like my beliefs are coming out now verbally, publicly. In this political climate you can no longer not be racist. You have to be anti-racist. This is just embarrassing, having this conversation, like you had to get here? You had to be, like, up front with the people you represent and tell them that you can't get behind Black Lives Matter because of 'the politics.' How does that sound? How would that make students feel safe? Like, wow! And the fact that you're bringing your personal beliefs and politics into being SGA president on the university's campus and you're like, 'You know what, fuck everybody else this is what I feel and only how I feel and my beliefs matter.'

And honestly, at this point if you can't be behind this student body and get this student body what it wants, hey, step down! Why should everybody else have to pay? It shouldn't be about losing followers and making everybody upset. This is human rights, baby. That's all people are asking for."

"You really think that by saying 'Black Lives Matter' people are gonna be like, 'Oh wait, I thought Stevie was Christian?' Like you really think Christians can't say 'Black lives Matter?' Do you not see churches saying, Black Lives Matter?"

"Come on. Here we are, once again digging up stuff just to be like, 'This is why I don't want to say, 'Black Lives Matter.' And this is why people are calling you racist, Stevie. This is the reason why. And honestly, to them, this is proof that you can't be behind black people and minority people on this campus. People are crying out. I'm asking myself in tears some nights what more can I do in this organization? How can I do my part? Stevie, do you understand what I'm saying? Does everyone on this call understand what I'm saying? Am I crazy? Stevie, in those messages you were honestly trying to gaslight me. I'm not crazy. We are on this call, and you

were saying these things, Stevie. Let the student body know. Write it out in a statement. We want honesty from you at this point. If you can't stand behind Black Lives Matter, let people know that. If that's really how you feel, why can't you let people know that? If this is truly your belief and you're going to stand strong in it, why can't you let people know that? That way people can then make their own opinions and decisions about you."

Stevie: *"I just want to say that we said this would be a predominately respectful call and I think it's a little upsetting. I don't appreciate having my religion being called a 'cop-out.' That's very upsetting because I have lost a lot of sleep over all this. I had Coronavirus when this was all happening, when I heard you were upset, Kevin. It's very upsetting because I know it's a very stressful time for us but..."*

Kevin: *"I wouldn't have brought up your Christianity if you didn't bring it up."*

Stevie: *"Okay, in regard to what you said in showing how we're against racism, I thought we were very clear on it. Not only did we speak on it being bad, but we* *also came up with this plan on what to do. I welcome anyone who is upset that you are talking about—I want them to reach out to us, SGA as a whole. I'm perfectly fine with putting it up to a vote because SGA is not just me, it's all these senators. I'd love to have it come up for a vote, but I thought I made it very clear that racism and discrimination are wrong."*

Kevin: *"You're saying that you don't realize that people are upset about it. Did you not check your social media? Did you not see the almost 400 comments? And back to the religion thing. You know, I grew up in Christianity. I went to private school. I still believe I'm a Christian and I say, 'Black Lives Matter.' What does this have to do with religion at all? You don't think if we're going there that Jesus would be for Black Lives Matter?"*

Stevie: *"I think He'd be against violence and racism and discrimination. He showed us He was. I've tried to be exactly like that, I've tried to be against violence, discrimination, anything that hurts any community I've always been against."*

Nathan: *"I think that we've reached a point where we all understand what's been said and there doesn't need*

to be any further clarification. The focus here, specifically from Kevin's side, is that the black community at
Belmont and the minority community. I'm not going
to name any brothers, but Kevin's spoken to me about
the brothers he's spoken to that are minority brothers,
alumni and current. They feel that they are all in congruence with this: it's that what needs to be said is
'Black Lives Matter.'"

Kevin: "Not to cut you off but I want to add on that.
Not even just minorities and black people. White
people too."

Mark: "And there you go. It's the movement that is
happening right now within the United States, everybody with a head on their shoulders is in agreement
that all lives matter, that racism is wrong. But what's
happening right now, if you think about this like, say
a familial table: everybody's eating food, right? And
you know there's black lives at one end. Everybody
else is getting a piece of the pie, [but] black people
aren't. Everybody's like, 'Oh all lives matter, everything counts! We don't believe in discrimination.' But
the problem is, black people, they're not getting their

piece of the pie. They're not observing the pie on their plate on their fork and into their mouth."

Kevin: *"All lives don't matter until black lives do."*

Mark: *"And so the point here is that what they want to hear — not just black people on campus but everybody that Kevin has talked to, of all races, are in agreement, that SGA needs specifically a statement from you, Stevie, which is why we're here. If this was about SGA we wouldn't be here. But this is about you being a member and representative of this brotherhood, as well as of this entire student body. And it's just that one statement. And, you know, denounce all the violence and acts against Christianity you want. As a Christian organization, we all agree Jesus would be for Black Lives Matter. And so, you know, it's a Christian organization. It's just students on campus who want to hear that, and they want to hear it from you. They view your first post as ignorant. And despite how you meant it, it's all about how it was perceived. How it was perceived was being insensitive. That's sort of where we're at."*

Logan: "*What it boils down to, Stevie, is everyone would love for you to release a statement that specifically says, 'Black Lives Matter.' And correct me Kevin if I'm wrong, but Black Lives Matter has begun and has stood for all minorities and everybody. And like we said, all lives matter once Black Lives Matter, that kind of thing. Saying that statement is more than just for the black students on campus, it's for the minorities and everyone involved. And by releasing that statement with those three words in it doesn't change your view of anyone other than it can help where you come from right now, because the silence or, I guess, lack of saying 'Black Lives Matter,' is perceived to be almost like against it, whether or not you agree with the political side which we discussed. You don't, and most people don't, agree with the political side of tearing down monuments and the acts of violence, and most people don't believe that. But the two have been linked together, so by saying that, Stevie, I get where you're coming from: saying 'No, I can't get behind an organization that does that.' But by saying 'Black Lives Matter,' it's not about politics and the organization like that. It's about the basic human rights affiliated; and people just want to hear you, or I guess you and SGA with your name on it, say 'Black Lives Matter' and mean it and put that out for everyone. And don't just say it to go through the motions. You gotta mean it and it's gotta be real. And that's what everyone's been hoping to get out of this and that's what Kevin's been kinda driving tonight: he wants you and SGA to say that because kind of by not it's that perception of, 'Is he for or against?' And yeah, your Instagram posts: while I understand where you're coming from, the perception of other people is that it was very poor timing and poor taste. The captions could've been significantly better and things like that. So, because of that, now you're looked at in a negative light by a lot of people that Kevin's been talking about. You've got a lot of this negative light currently, so by releasing this 'Black Lives Matter' statement that you mean and have everyone on the same page with, it's going to make people go, 'Okay, yeah, maybe he was naive or foolish with his Instagram posts, but now we are aware he is for us. He supports us, he wants the best for us, and he is going to support this movement.' And not the burnings and the lootings and the crimes and stuff, but the actual human respect and decency that everyone deserves is what they're hoping to get out of this. We can all agree what you meant that first post to be, but unfortunately nobody else understands or sees it that way."*

Nathan: "So this is very much a lead by example thing. Although SGA has come out with some statements—you know, recognizing Juneteenth, and then your initial statements standing with minority communities and being against racism— the community at Belmont doesn't feel that you align. And your silence, unfortunately, has shown that you don't. What they're calling for is you to be the example, to be the outspoken leader of the entire Belmont student community, saying 'I believe Black Lives Matter,' saying, 'SGA believes Black Lives Matter.' It seems like what you said, being against racism, you would believe that. I understand your hesitation and your being against what the leaders of the political organization said: that they have taken and titled 'Black Lives Matter.' Some of the things that have happened have been atrocious. But that's not the point. The point of this is that you're standing with the community, the black community. It's 6:40 now, say we've got 20 minutes. What we're looking for is some sort of action point, some commitment to action. If we can't get it after this meeting, it sort of leaves our hands tied at that point and, you know, if you can't recognize that, then that puts us in a very tough spot."

"Kevin has been very clear what he's going to do should you not make a statement aligning yourself with black lives and every minority community. Like he said, he's not asking you personally to make any monetary donations or any statements on your personal page. This is about representing the university's community and saying, 'Hey, what's going on is wrong and we're with you.' If you can think of barring any personal feelings as far as against the Christian community or anything like that, if you can think of some solution that is reasonable, we would love to hear it. Unfortunately, if you put us in a tough position, then you're going to put yourself in a tough position, and you're going to put Kevin in a tough position where he feels like he's going to have to make a public statement saying, 'Hey, Stevie doesn't actually support us.' And it's going to spiral out of control very fast. It doesn't seem like you want that."

"You are a genuinely kind person. Every person you meet you try to treat with kindness. You try to treat people equally. So, you know, at this point we would like to hear what you think would be an appropriate response. And please take your time to think about it..."

Kevin: *"I just want to add two more things. As for the Fourth of July post and, you know, saying, making captions like that? It wasn't, I think it was a known, like, a generalized thing this year in America that, you know, we're not going to post anything controversial when it comes to the Fourth of July. We want to stand with Black Lives Matter this year. We know a lot of the Founding Fathers weren't for black people. So that's what I meant when I said we want to 'tie them down,' because most things that are generalized ain't got like — we want them to celebrate Fourth of July the same as we always do, as a country. And then, secondly, I also wanted to bring up this point because I know you said you couldn't stand Black Lives Matter and you could not get with that statement or that political organization."*

"My question is: if that's true, why are you still in the fraternity, because we made two statements and if you don't believe in that shouldn't you no longer associate yourself with the organization? Just a thought. And like I said, at the end of the day, if you say, 'You know what, I'm going to stand firm in my stance. I'm not going to say, "Black Lives Matter" and these are my reasons why.' Stevie, I think you owe it to everybody

in the student body to let them know that. Don't hide behind — don't be a coward about it. Like, if that's how you feel, say it. Because at the end of the day, I cannot make you say, 'Black Lives Matter.' And when no one in this conversation can forcibly make you or SGA say 'Black Lives Matter' but the people — if you can't get behind it because of politics and religion, just say that and let people know. "Cause you know, that's just the truth. And you know what? At the end of the day, yeah, it's just so upsetting that you truly, truly feel that way and I hope in the future you can dig down deep and see your errors."

Stevie: *"I just have a question. I know that Nathan — I guess we can wait for him to come back — he called me, and he told me that, his exact quote was that you were going to do 'whatever it took to destroy me.' I'm just very worried. That's what he said. I'm feeling a little bit like—I don't want to be threatened or any-thing like that—and that's what it sounded like when he was talking."*

Kevin: *"Stevie, I didn't threaten you. I wanted you to hear it directly from the horse's mouth."*

Stevie: "He said that you were going to do certain things. I'm just upset by that a little bit because I feel like that's threatening, blackmail. I just don't appreciate that."

Kevin: "Blackmail? I think it's funny you're bringing this up now when you had all this time. If this was truly a thing that happened, then I think I would have jotted this down as one of my main points. 'Kevin, he's going to do whatever it takes to destroy me.' Destroy you? Stevie, come on."

Stevie: "That's what he told me when he called me. He said you were going to post things and it was going to destroy my career. That's what he told me."

Kevin: "As far as threatening goes: Stevie, do you truly know what it feels like to be threatened? Imagine being threatened because of the color of your skin. Let's highlight that for a second."

At this point, the meeting turned into a discussion of who said what when. It seemed clear to me that people were trying to cover their tracks and get their stories straight. It wasn't easy for me to sit there and keep silent when Stevie's accusers were calling him a liar and a coward because he wasn't telling the truth as they saw it, when it was clear that they weren't being truthful.

> *Nathan:* *"Let me put some context on this. So, when this was initially brought to me, I spoke to Stevie. I was like, 'Hey, people are calling for you to acknowledge 'Black Lives Matter.' I said, 'What has been stated is that they're going to do what it takes to call you out and essentially what's going to happen is it's going to bring you down and there's no two ways about that, right?' And that didn't come out of you, destroying his reputation, that did not come out of his mouth. But that's essentially what would happen..."*

> *Stevie:* *"Isn't that what you said though, Nathan?"*

> *Kevin:* *"But can I highlight that really quick? I don't know exactly what you said, Nathan, but even for you to directly say I was talking to you out of confidence and with you as risk manager on Standards..."*

> *Nathan:* *"This is way before you referred him."*

> *Kevin:* *"No, it wasn't!"*

Nathan: "No, no, no no no. This is earlier in the summer. This is when you first expressed —"

Kevin: "Nathan, the first time I talked to you was what, last week? I have not talked to you since. Wait, where is this coming from?"

Nathan: "This isn't—this is when you brought it to Kyle, who brought it to me."

Kevin: "This is getting past — see, see, you see where the issue is here? This is why I don't talk to Kyle, literally, on racism. That was like 'telephone' and some indirect information getting spread around."

Nathan: "Kevin, let me finish. I'm sorry. Look, you brought some concerns to Kyle about Stevie. You said, 'I don't believe Stevie is acting concurrently with what he's saying.' You felt he wasn't acting like a true brother. Kyle said, 'Hey look, Kevin brought this concern to me, you're on Standards. I need you to do something,' essentially."

"I went to Stevie, I said, 'Hey look, there are people who feel you are not acting in congruence with what you *believe.' I said, 'Kevin, one of our brothers, he's brought up concerns about your post. He feels like you need to have some action acknowledging Black Lives Matter. He wants to take it public if you're not willing to take any action. And he wants to make it known that you aren't who you were claiming to be.' I said—and this may have gotten lost in translation—"There are people who don't want to see you representing the student body. Basically, if you don't make this statement it's going to be very hard for people to justify wanting you to be their representative.' I said, 'It's going to bring you down to ruin your reputation, and it's going to effectively destroy you and what you want."*

Kevin: *"That's perfectly fine with me. Everything that I have said in the past was in that referral that I sent to Standards. I don't know what all this 'lost in translation' was going for. I'll say what I gotta say and I did not threaten you. Like Stevie, read the over 300 comments by the student body, and you feel threatened by me, Stevie? You think I'm the only one on campus that feels the way I do, that suddenly that threatens you? This is some clown shit, y'all."*

Nathan: "Kevin, Kevin we all believe you. We understand where you're coming from."

Kevin: "Now I'm not even mad at you. I'm just mad at Stevie because, Stevie, you're already trying to say I threatened you. Now I'm going to go start something that ain't even true."

Logan: "I'm just saying one thing: this whole conversation is based on people's different perceptions...and we're trying to understand everyone's perceptions here."

Nathan: "Let's clear the air now. Stevie, Kevin is your brother. Kevin is only here to call you to a higher standard. That's why he referred you to Standards. The point is to only bring you up. Based on our conversation earlier in the summer, clearly, I didn't communicate well, and I'll take responsibility for that. That could be absolutely on me. I don't remember exactly what was said."

"As I explained when I summarized just now, that's what my intentions were: to portray to you, Stevie. Kevin doesn't want to bring you down or threaten you or harm you. All Kevin wants to do is call you to that

higher standard, to be aligned with what we as the fraternity have released as a statement twice, saying what we align with. Just to give you a little history on our bylaws: our bylaws allow for Standards to hold any brother accountable who isn't acting as a fraternity man: ethically, morally, based on the creed, anything of that nature. It doesn't have to be a specific action, that's in the bylaws. What Kevin has cited is that your inaction, your lack of voice Black Lives Matter has shown that you are not in alignment with what we are saying as a fraternity. And so, where we're at now with the five minutes we have left — and then Stevie's gotta bounce. So, either we commit to a solution within the next five minutes, we call again to make a solution, or you talk it out and then it's eventually going to come back to us to make a decision because Stevie, if you can't align with what we've said, we have to have a much more serious conversation".

Logan: "This amplifies to a much higher level. If you cannot agree with this kind of stuff. This goes way up on our radar."

Nathan: "I'd like to reiterate that you've already stated you're against racism and that you're against *the immoral actions that have occurred. You know, nobody here is not in alliance with that. We all agree with that, including Kevin. And all Kevin is asking is for you to just be more vocal and release another statement. Work with him. Stevie, you have already reached out to Kevin asking for his suggestions in wanting to meet with him. These are his suggestions. And if you're going to take him seriously as a representative of the fraternity, which is the most important thing for this conversation, then do it."*

As I said previously, it was extremely difficult for me to stay quiet throughout this meeting, watching, and listening as my son was treated as if he were a lawbreaker who deserved to be punished, simply because he insisted on standing up for his values and beliefs.

Remember that prior to the meeting, Stevie had been assured that it would be for the purpose of bringing him and Kevin together so they could discuss their opinions and come to an agreement—but that was a lie. There was no room for Stevie's opinion, and he was expected to conform – or else.

I watched every look on my son's face and could do nothing but sit in silence through the circus trial as the student in charge unleashed a mob on him. Stevie was not allowed to speak much but told what he "had to do" to be able to stay in the fraternity.

Shame on these young men, the future of our country, being so rude, unfair, and kowtowing to one student instead of keeping their word to also meet Stevie's needs.

Several of the members spoke over Stevie with their claims that: "BLM is not a political organization" and "White silence is violence." The worst of it all came from Kevin, the so-called "brother" who targeted Stevie with trumped-up charges of not meeting their fraternity's Standards. He gaslit Stevie as the other members watched, all the while playing the victim as the only black member of their fraternity.

They knew he had threatened to destroy Stevie's reputation by going public and falsely labeling him a racist. Isn't that the card all the radical, destructionist left plays on Christian conservatives when they don't have truth on their side: defamation? I sat in disbelief and horror that these boys pretending to be men were calling themselves friends of my son, much less his brothers.

I was disgusted that we'd approved of this university and him being in this fraternity. Of course, with only one fraternity to choose from, there was not much of a choice. I am not a fraternity or sorority person myself, but we were assured by the administration this would be a "good experience" for Stevie as this was a "Conservative Christian University."

It seemed as though the administration was working hand-in-hand with the liberal mob to prevent any possibility of liberal discomfort. These awful feelings choked me up as I attempted to process everything going on in front of me. They told Stevie to craft a letter saying, 'Black Lives Matter' and mean it, or the fraternity would vote against his character as a brother. I knew Stevie would never do either. I raised a Christian who would never condone a group that was rioting, killing, and destroying cities, schools, and people.

I could tell by his stunned look that Stevie was very upset with the treatment by his brothers and in disbelief that the chair would allow him to be treated this way. His religion and character were called into question. I feared what these boys were capable of — I didn't recognize them anymore. They were angry. Two-faced. Hurtful. They didn't care about Stevie's values. They were trying to bend him to their will, even if it broke him.

6

ET TU, BRUTE?

After he clicked off from the Zoom call, Stevie was in shock. He sat there for a moment, staring at the blank screen in front of him, trying to make sense of what had just happened. A meeting that had been promoted as an opportunity to bring two fraternity brothers together so they could discuss their differences of opinion in a neutral and supportive atmosphere, had turned into a vicious attack on my son. The attack was launched by young men he considered his inner circle: his best friends, even. How and why had they turned on him like this?

I can't even say Stevie was angry—but I certainly was. I couldn't let them get away with this! I had to fight back! (And I believe that any mom who is reading this will know exactly how I felt.)

After thinking about it for a while, Stevie looked at me and asked, "What just happened?"

"You just found what it's like to be betrayed," I told him. The only thing I had to be thankful for was that my son's "brothers" hadn't been carrying daggers that day. Otherwise, the whole thing might have ended up as a much too lifelike reenactment of the assassination of Julius Caesar.

Finally, after some time spent processing the unexpected events of the day, Stevie phoned Nathan to voice his disbelief concerning the way he had been treated on the Zoom call.

When Nathan heard Stevie's voice, he acted as if nothing was wrong, and asked what I thought was a really dumb question, "How are you doing?"

"Well, you know I'm not gonna lie man," Stevie answered. "I'm a little bit upset; he [Kevin] came after me pretty hard. You know, we agreed that we were not going to be attacking each other. I just want you to know that wasn't right, that was wrong. I'm a little bit disappointed."

"I understand that" Nathan said, "and I sympathize with you. I'm sorry you feel that he attacked you...As your Big, I don't want to see that happen to you, but because I'm on Standards I sort of have to be very impartial."

He went on, "Unfortunately as a group we feel that Kevin's stance is actually very reasonable, and we didn't perceive him as attacking you. More so, we saw that what he wanted is just for you to make that statement. If there was anything that really rubbed you the wrong way, then you're right we should have stopped that. Of course, that's on us."

He paused for a moment and then went on.

"What happened happened, and I'm sorry you feel a little let down. We just—what we want is a solution where, you know. You're not being called out publicly as being a racist. We all know that you're not, and we want a solution where you feel comfortable. We feel like that's a really good start."

Obviously, Nathan still didn't see that Stevie had been mistreated, or that the members of the fraternity had mistreated him. Or, if he did, he wasn't about to admit it.

Stevie explained that he felt that Kevin and the other members of the fraternity were trying to intimidate him into doing something he didn't really want to do, but, naturally, Nathan didn't see it that way.

"Trust me," he said, "tough spots are what Standards are made of right now. We have a lot of referrals about a lot of different things. We're all having to make some really tough calls and decisions, so we're sort of — I mean, this meeting is one of many that we have to have. But it's not just this one topic; there's so much going on for us."

When the subject of the fraternity endorsement of Black Lives Matter came up, Stevie explained, "I was of the mind that you can disagree but still be part of something. But unfortunately, it seems that the fraternity isn't of the same opinion."

Nathan agreed. "Yeah, unfortunately we have released two statements on Black Lives Matter..."

"Not only that," Stevie interrupted, "but it was also an endorsement of the organization. You even had their logo and website address on screen."

Nathan seemed surprised.

"We had the website up?" he asked.

"Yes," Stevie told him. "It was on the last page of the Instagram post."

How could Nathan NOT know what the fraternity was supporting? How could he support something that he clearly didn't even know about? But he insisted that he didn't know about this, and added, "I'm 100 percent confident that none of the rest of us in Standards know about it either."

He went on, "None of us agree with any of the violence that's happening, any of the awful things that they're doing, any of that. So, you know, people who are using 'Black Lives Matter' as an excuse to be violent, we think that's awful. We've had conversations like that on Standards. We're all in congruence with no racism, Black Lives Matter, all lives matter... we all believe in the equal treatment of everybody. We on Standards have all confirmed that to each other so that we know where we stand. I love you and I wanna protect you, but you know I gotta walk a fine line here and as a member of Standards, I can't let my personal feelings get in the way of the decisions that we make."

I felt like my head was about to explode because the conversation was going in circles. Nathan seemed to understand Stevie's perspective up to a point, but it always came back to, "I can't let my personal feelings get in the way."

"Well, there's just one other thing I want to talk to you about," Stevie explained. "I'm getting to the point where I'm very nervous. There have been threats made. Campus security is involved, and I have to meet with them. It sounds like someone in our own fraternity is threatening me. You told me over the phone: you said, 'They're going to do whatever it takes to destroy you.'"

"No, no," Nathan replied. "I didn't mean that anyone was going to destroy you physically. Nothing like that. I was talking about your reputation. They want to make you look bad. They want your image destroyed. I hate that it was perceived as physical because that's not what it was about at all."

Nathan tried to soothe Stevie's feelings by again apologizing that he "felt" attacked. From my point of view, his feelings about the situation were 100 percent correct. He didn't "feel" like he had been attacked. He had been attacked! Not only that. He had been sandbagged as well. He was asked to come to a meeting that was supposed to be a friendly discussion, and then set upon by wolves who wanted to tear him apart!

"I know this was a long conversation tonight," Nathan said. "A lot of things were said, and I can understand that you feel you were attacked. That's not what we wanted and I'm sorry you felt ganged up on. That was not the intention."

Stevie shook his head. "Maybe so. But that's what happened."

It was time for Nathan to take off his "good-cop hat" and put on his "bad-cop" version.

"I know," he said. "And you know what, we're sorry. That's on us and I can apologize for that. But what I need to make clear is that you are a representative of the fraternity and unfortunately if you don't make a statement saying that you're against racism—we believe that where you're at right now, the steps that you're taking right? This is an amazing start, but this is something that's going to have to happen. Unfortunately, the fraternity has aligned themselves. It's going to put us in a really, really hard position if we have to make a decision on your character because you haven't aligned yourself with the fraternity. Does that make sense? Standards aren't asking you to align yourself with a political organization. At all. We actually prefer that you don't."

"But you guys did," Stevie protested.

Nathan disagreed. "We don't align ourselves with a political organization. At least, not Standards."

"But you just said that the fraternity posted the Black Lives Matter website on Instagram. You just said, how it applies to me, it applies the same to that political organization. You said it. You said you don't agree with the political organization, I don't either. Does that mean we should both be kicked out? Because that's what the fraternity endorsed. Everyone on that call, by that logic, you should be kicked out."

I could tell that Nathan was frustrated. That was because Stevie was in the right. He was being held to a double standard.

"That's fair," he said. But that's not the important thing to recognize here. The important thing being recognized here is what Kevin asked of you. Kevin has said that he doesn't even agree with the violent actions of the organization or the political abuse of human rights. He stands against it: he stated it on his call to Standards. That's sort of where we're at. I don't agree with the organization, but I said to Kevin that I agree, Black Lives Matter. I understand that the huge catalyst here for you is that the organization itself and some of the things that they've done, which I agree are atrocious and awful. I have very strong feelings about anybody that attacks Christ as a person. You know where I stand on it. I'm just trying to make it clear that you are not being asked to support the organization but to say that you believe in Black Lives Matter.

You're not believing in the organization; you just believe in fundamental human equal rights. Does it make sense?"

Stevie was not about to roll over and play dead. "No," he said, "because that is the name of the organization. That's literally the name. He said I had to say those words. Racism is wrong. But Black Lives Matter, that's the name of the organization. That's the issue."

Nathan's response to this was, "We're on the same page."

Really? It didn't sound like it to me, or to Stevie.

Nathan went on, "I think the main thing here is that you're going to have to involve Kevin in crafting a statement. All that they're asking is that you align yourself with a statement from SGA. What they see is that you're a big organization and that you're the representative for that organization and the student body. That's how they see it. So, I understand that if you guys have to go to vote, do it. But as long as Kevin sees that you're making progress, making next steps. Then we have to make a decision on what's going to happen…I know you feel personally accountable for Belmont and what happens on campus, so I know you're going to do the best work. This is just going to be a process and something we work through."

Below, I am posting the endorsement for Black Lives Matter that the fraternity posted on their Instagram page. I would think it was voted on but that is making an assumption.

If these young men aren't following rules for what they are supposedly believing — Lord, help us:

> Lastly, we implore you to do what you can to support local, Black-owned businesses in this time and research the Black Lives Matter movement by checking out their website at www.blacklivesmatter.com. We realize these words would mean nothing without any action behind them. In honor of the ongoing troubles, our chapter will be donating to the Nashville Bail Fund and is actively looking to donate to more organizations. We encourage you to also take action through donations, social media, peacefully protesting, signing petitions, calling local government officials, and more. We firmly believe all lives can't matter until Black lives matter. We will continue to do our part fighting for the Black Lives Matter movement and using our privilege to fight for more seats at the table.

"Lastly, we implore you to do what you can to support local, Black-owned businesses in this time and research the Black Lives Matter Movement by checking out their website at www.blacklivesmatter.com. We realize that these words would mean nothing without any action behind them. In honor of the ongoing troubles, our chapter will be donating to the Nashville Bail Fund and is actively looking to donate to more organizations. We encourage you to also take action through donations, social media, peacefully protesting, signing petitions, calling local government officials, and more. We

firmly believe all lives can't matter until Black Lives Matter. We will continue to do our part fighting for the Black Lives Matter movement and using our privilege to fight for more seats at the table."

That was the end of the call. No real resolution there, even though Nathan admitted that the fraternity was wrong to post and endorse BLM, and that their Standards Committee had ganged up on Stevie. Nathan even admitted to knowing that Stevie was facing threats of violence — but did he offer any help? No. Just empty apologies.

With the threats of violence persisting and the fraternity only adding further pressure on him, Stevie decided to take up his case with higher powers. He requested a meeting with the SGA advisor and the Greek Life representative They met five days later on September 1.

When they did, Stevie recounted everything that had happened to him: the harassment, the threats, and the accusations bordering on defamation. He was clear that he wanted it all to stop and that they were the ones who could stop it. Stevie explained how tired he was of being slandered by the fraternity and cited his rights from the student handbook.

I initially felt good about the meeting, because I believed that these people heard what Stevie was saying, and that they could finally do something. Other students were being protected for far less, so why not Stevie?

Stevie was relieved when the Greek Life representative said she was upset with the Fraternity Standards Board. Her reaction convinced him that something would be done. But again, empty apologies.

Ultimately, he was turned away without any concrete solutions. Belmont never did anything to the fraternity members or organizations for threatening Stevie. The fraternity remained on campus. A few months later, they even hired Kevin as their event and venue coordinator, but never punished him for his threatening behavior.

After spending some time thinking about what he should do, and praying for the Lord's guidance, Stevie felt he had no choice but to make a clean break. Rather than be kicked out of the fraternity for refusing to endorse BLM, he decided to act against a group of people who hated him and the way he felt about America. The next day, September 2, he dropped his membership from the fraternity.

He was surprised that not one of the three entities to which he was required to send his withdrawal form reached out to him. Not the fraternity. Not national headquarters. Nor the campus life office. I couldn't help but feel more and more disgusted as the days went by. I wondered if they all turned a blind eye because they thought Stevie might stir up the same level of drama as all the BLM activist students had done.

Although they were aware of his stress, Stevie was hung out to dry. Out of curiosity, I checked Belmont's student handbook. Policy dictated that all three of the entities should have reached out to him. My suspicions were confirmed. Perhaps it was for the best: they didn't even have the wherewithal to follow their own rules. How could I expect them to protect my son?

Even though none of the three entities reached out to Stevie, other Belmont officials did. On September 3, the SGA advisor sent Stevie an email, informing him that Belmont's legal team and two others, who were attorneys for the school, were supportive of Stevie's case. However, he said that this trio needed all the specific information and credible threats Stevie had received.

Hello Stevie —
I reached out to   They are both supportive. With that said, they both stated that we will need specific information on what you feel like has gotten out of hand any specific and credible threats you have received. If you have any of that information, let me know and I can pass that forward.

Thanks!

Hello Stevie-

I reached out to [the lawyers]. They are both supportive. With that said, they both stated that we will need specific information on what you feel like has

gotten out of hand any specific and credible threats
you have received. If you have any of that information,
let me know and I can pass that forward.

Thanks!

Once again, Stevie went to work compiling evidence. He sent them the email petition that had been posted against him, along with the Instagram account made with his likeness as well as the comments made multiple times online about how people would attack him if they saw him on campus. He also included copies of threatening emails, transcripts from Zoom meetings, etc. It seemed to me that this was more than enough evidence to show what Stevie had been put through, but the attorneys thought otherwise.

What more of a smoking gun were they looking for? Stevie was still not safe. The fraternity Zoom call alone broke many rules, yet the school and the advisor refused to act.

While the administration did not feel that this was enough to get involved, it only took a few days for Nathan to realize the mistake he was making. Perhaps it was his conscience that had finally enlightened him, although we will never know. I was just relieved that Stevie was no longer a part of this dysfunctional two-faced group of young men who the university allowed to run wild. On September 5, Nathan left Stevie a voicemail just before midnight:

> *"Hey buddy. It's your boy, Nathan. I know it's late, sorry for calling you late, I know you probably got work in the morning. I know there's school tomorrow, I hope the transition back to in-person learning goes well for you. I just wanted to call and just talk to you about something I guess I've been thinking about for a little while. It's been sitting on my heart and something I've been praying about. I don't think the last time we spoke after Standards and stuff like that, that I did a good job of hearing what you had to say. I honestly just don't feel like I've been there for you like I should have been as a friend and as a Big, it's been wild and crazy. So, yeah, just wanted to apologize for that. Love to talk to you and catch up. Just see how you're doing and just talk about school and shoot shit and catch up. Another thing I wanted to say is that I think it was — you brought up a good point about how we have posted a link to the Black Lives Matter website and how we have been sort of calling you to stand with what the fraternity has set. But obviously that's wrong because you're not going to support any political organization like that. And especially one that's*

made an assault on the values that you hold, that we both hold. I'm working on that, and I agree it's wrong. I don't think we did a good job of hearing you. Like I said earlier. All that aside, at this point, all that's sort of behind us. On the other side, I just want to talk to you and hang out like friends and catch up. How's it going? Hope classes are going better, I know Zoom was kind of hard. I hope in-person goes better for you. Love you brother, bye."

Too little, too late. What do you call a friend who won't stand beside you in public?

The fraternity refused to admit that Black Lives Matter was a political organization. When they made it clear they were willing for Stevie — no, requiring him — to give up his convictions to align with the status quo, Nathan was complicit.

That one BLM mantra kept echoing in my head: "White silence is violence."

7
LIES, DECEIT AND INDIFFERENCE

From the time he was a very young boy, Stevie had always had a calm spirit that came from his understanding that God is in control. When I got uptight or worried about anything, he was likely to remind me that the Bible says, in the book of Romans, "in all things, God works for the good of those who love Him." (Romans 8:28 NIV)

Don't get me wrong. He has always believed in taking reasonable precautions. We both feel that God wants us to do what we can, but to understand that the outcome is in His hands.

So, since he knew God was in control, Stevie decided to go back to in-person classes as the glorious month of September came to its colorful conclusion. He telephoned campus police on September 21 and talked to a school police captain who told him that he did not need an escort any longer because, supposedly, people had forgotten about him by then. Clearly, Belmont still had done nothing about the threats or the fraternity at that point.

Feeling that Stevie was getting the runaround, I called the officer who I had previously talked to during the summer, and an assistant. The officer claimed that he had spoken with Stevie on the phone. He also told me that Stevie had agreed to come into the campus police office the next day at 8:30 a.m. I was confused because Stevie had not mentioned any such meeting with me. We were very careful and intentional with all things Belmont. Stevie and I were on the same page with calls, meetings, etc, to ensure his safety. I was the one making the call to this officer since the captain felt Stevie was not in any harm's way, so why was I told that Stevie had already spoken with him? Well, imagine my surprise when I found out the officer lied to me. Stevie had never gotten a call from him. Our phone records showed no missed call. Now, even campus security was no longer looking out for my son. This was such a disappointment that I can't even begin to put it into words.

I called a contact in campus police, and she knew right away that I was livid. I felt that I had every reason to be angry. I'd caught the campus police in a lie, and that lie had scary implications for my son! It was apparent more than ever at that point: even the administration was discriminating against Stevie. She recalled being on the call in the summer where Stevie and I were told he would have security and she would see to it that he did, however, she said that he still wouldn't be allowed to have his car on campus at any time. If he parked on campus, she said it would not be the responsibility of Belmont's to assure the car was safe. To say I was stunned is an understatement. These edicts were discouraging him from even attending class. I told her not to worry about the car, as Stevie would be there one way or another — but his safety was still a huge concern of ours.

Despite the lies and indifference, Stevie didn't feel deterred from living his senior year to his fullest. On September 24, he went back to in-person classes for the first time. He came up with a plan: park at a friend's garage three blocks away. Then, a friend would pick him up and drive him to campus police so he could be escorted to class as pictured below.

Contrary to what campus police claimed, Belmont's students did recognize him. How could they not? His picture continued to be plastered all over social media. He was subjected to name-calling and whispered threats. These young, presumably Christian, Belmont students were acting like the worst bullies from junior high school.

That same day, the SGA advisor had a Zoom call with Stevie and his Vice President. He told them there was no need to have SGA meetings all semester. He said there was nothing for them to do during COVID-19—yet there was an upcoming Presidential Debate in less than a month. How were they supposed to fulfill their obligations as SGA President and Vice President if they had no meetings? That was the whole point of their election. They were barred from representing the student body. I understood that the campus authorities were doing their very best to keep Stevie out of the way and appease the activists. I remember Stevie remarking to me, "We're being censored by Belmont."

Stevie and his VP were promised full access to planning, doing interviews, meeting the Presidential candidates, and attending the Debate. They repeatedly tried to reach out to the two student chairs for direction as instructed in Belmont's emails to students but got no response. Stevie texted with the student chair in charge. He told Stevie that one of his peers was supposed to have reached out to Stevie and his Vice President, but she never did.

A few days later, Stevie had a phone call with another dean at Belmont. In this call, Stevie talked to her about ways that SGA could help students feel that their voices were being heard on campus and being properly represented. Stevie wanted to work with an organization that helped at-risk children in Nashville and throughout Tennessee, but she told him that it would not help the situation and that unless he endorsed Black Lives Matter the torrent of abuse would not cease and she seemed quite proud of this. She also told Stevie that "Tensions are high because of the election but they will go down soon."

I was rather upset with this dean because of the way she dismissed Stevie and shot down his ideas for making a positive difference in the community. Instead of helping him, she wanted him to bow to the mob if he wanted this to stop, and she made it seem like he was the true villain for supporting the United States of America. When she and I spoke, she took a very different tone with me and told me that my son was part of the problem and that she wanted to "school both Stevie and I on what the true meaning of the 4th of July is, as Stevie is a racist" and I was "not properly educated on the true meaning of the 4th of July." She extended an invitation for Stevie and me to come to her office and be taught why the United States is a racist nation and that anyone who supports it is in fact a racist themself. She also said that the 4th of July was not a holiday celebrated by everyone as "Only white people were free, black people were still slaves." I told her that she was confusing the 4th of July with the Emancipation Proclamation signed by Republican President

Abraham Lincoln. This crossed every boundary with me, and I could no longer hold my tongue. I told her that I attended a top 100 nationally ranked university, that I had done well there, and if she thought Stevie didn't understand the meaning of the 4th then perhaps her university, a non-nationally ranked one, is to blame. Then I told her I was terminating this conversation as it was going to go nowhere. I was shaking as I hung up the phone. I wondered how this angry, hate-filled woman had come to be employed at a conservative Christian university.

A very wise man named Mr. Herman Cain once told me that I can only help those who are open to hearing the truth, but I need to let the ones who are ignorant to the truth go. It was one of the best conversations of my life and I drew strength from that. Following Mr. Cain's advice, I never spoke with this woman again. I was highly insulted by this dean and could hear the hate in her voice. I am a Christian woman. I will not hate but I also will not waste my time with someone who has prejudged my family. Stevie, too, never met with her.

8

THE COLLEGE BLACKSHIRTS

On October 11th, Stevie attended a political event in Williamson County. Rob Smith, a notable black gay conservative, was speaking at the event along with Robby Starbuck and other conservatives. The event was hosted by the Republican County Party and our family wanted to go and welcome Rob Smith to Williamson County.

There were hundreds of people at this outdoor event in downtown Franklin, including many liberal protestors, who organized a "Honk-A-Thon" to drown out the speeches of Rob Smith, Robby Starbuck, and our county party chair. Many of the speakers in attendance were conservative minorities, and many of the protesters were students that Stevie knew. In fact, they had all posted on their accounts that they would be there and shared the flier of the planned protest. They called it the Honk-A-Thon.

Upon my arrival at the Republican rally, I noticed cars parked in the lot and dozens of students milling around the park. Many of these cars had BLM posters in their windows. The local police, sheriff and deputies were there as well, and seemed to be trying to keep the students away from the main stage. But I must wonder to this day — why were they there? I have attended many gatherings with these same speakers and never once have these students been at any of our events. Why this one?

I even recognized some of the protesters as students who had sent emails and made Instagram comments calling for violence against Stevie. I am grateful to our law enforcement officers for keeping things peaceful, but I wondered if there would come a time when there was no sheriff and security and Stevie would be alone, surrounded by the haters?

A few days later, while all this was going on, Stevie participated with four other Republicans in the university's College Republican and College Democrat Debate on Zoom. Initially, he planned to moderate the debate with two other members of his cabinet. But because of what was happening on campus, he decided that it was time to go on the attack and educate these socialists on why America is the land of opportunity.

Since this was a public debate on Zoom, I watched as Stevie and the other College Republicans were shouted down and called racists because they supported American values. One female student on the Democratic side was of particular interest, as she cut off the College Republicans and consistently interrupted anytime she did not agree with something. She also cut off the Democratic male students, implying that this was a debate where only young women should be heard.

I think one of the most frightening things was seeing the facial reactions of students who looked so angry and hateful. In fact, I recognized one of the girls from this debate. She was one of those who had been screaming and yelling, trying to prevent Rob Smith and Robby Starbuck from being heard when they hosted their rally just a few days prior.

Stevie tried to keep the debate on point. After all, it was supposed to be a civil discourse, not a hate fest. He addressed the matter of the Trump Tax Cuts:

"Under the Trump Tax cuts, families of 4 receive a tax break of $2,000," he said. "As a result of President Trump's strong business background and lifting 7 million people off of food stamps, our GDP rose by 3 percent. We replaced NAFTA with the USMCA with both candidates agreeing with it. Joe Biden said a few weeks ago that he would have supported the USMCA. Many in Congress have suggested that increased taxes and more government regulations are bad for the economy and bad for the people of America. Look at the Affordable Care act. More government intervention slows economic recovery."

Andrew, who also is a conservative, added: "Look at what the Trump tax cuts did for the American public. They gave us record low unemployment rates at 3.5 percent and, in the African American community 5.4 percent as well. If you look and compare that to what happened under the Obama-Biden Administration, they caused the slowest economic recovery since World War II because of the Affordable Care Act and the increase in taxes."

Stevie picked up on this: "During World War II, it was America's duty to defend freedom around the world, especially with the rise of Fascism in Europe, which we defeated, and then Communism, which took over the entire East. I think that America is a beacon of freedom and hope through capitalism to all of our allies and those in the former Soviet Union."

"America's role is to defend freedom for all people, but we need to do it in a way that keeps Americans safe and I think that President Trump has done a great job of doing this by taking troops out of the Middle East and forming partnerships with countries that have never gotten along, including the United Arab Emirates and Israel, which are now seeking to have peace without foreign intervention".

Arthur, also a Conservative said: "In addition, I think we should be leaders globally in protecting religious freedoms throughout the world."

The College Democrats had nothing to say about any of the facts Stevie and his team were presenting. Instead, they steered the debate to the subjects of racism and hatred.

Roger, a Democrat who was not signed up to speak, jumped in with a question: "If I may pose a question to the Republicans who claim that systematic racism does not exist, can you expand on that please? Can anyone respond to the systemic racism question?"

Andrew, who spoke earlier on the effectiveness of the Trump tax cuts, responded with, "More training, more equipment, and more resources for cops. Cops overall are very positive for our community. Yes, there are some bad ones just as there are some bad teachers and there are some bad students, and there's some bad people in every single thing in the world. We're not going to fight racism by taking funds away from the police. Unlike the Department of Education, allocating funds to the police would actually benefit them. There was an issue, where now most police departments require cameras which is great, but it would never have happened without funding."

He went on: "In addition, statistics show that 52 percent of African American people in a Gallup poll said that they want more police in their neighborhoods and 81 percent of people from a Gallup poll in 2019 said they do not want fewer police. I think that this is pretty important to take into consideration, since someone said that every single African American person is scared of the police."

The only reaction to this statement was strange facial expressions and calling him a "Chad" in the chat bar. Many alleged that Andrew did not attend Belmont when in fact, he was in his senior year and a close friend of Stevie's.

Once again, the Republicans tried to keep the debate about many topics, and Stevie answered a question about whether to increase the minimum wage. He explained it this way: "If there are three people paid $10 an hour, that's a total of $30 for one hour's work. If the government comes in and requires $15 per hour, then one of those people is likely to lose his or her job and will be making $0 per hour. So, obviously that person will be worse off than before, and the others will have to work harder than before to accomplish the same amount of work."

"Then if $15 is the minimum wage rather than letting the market determine fair prices, the price of bread is going to go up to $5 or $6. The price of rent will go up as well, as will groceries, clothes, and other items. Some people will make more in the short term, yet they will have to spend more, so they won't make any real gains."

Andrew chimed in with: "The minimum wage was never intended to have someone support themselves on it. It was meant for students and young adults who were starting out in their careers."

Following this, the left again went back to its red-flag issue of racism. A student named Stephanie said: "We need people to stop dying and we need black people to stop dying and stop being targeted by systemic racism. And we need people to understand that just because you think you are not racist and you don't have a racist ideology, that doesn't mean you're not. Take a sociology class at Belmont. I really encourage that. It's going to take more than me saying that."

Ashley, a Democrat participant in the debate, thought of a novel way to present her case: "I can say right now, if it makes everyone feel better, that I'm a racist. We're all racist." The other Democrats in the crowd seemed to agree with this. They went wild in the chat bar, and this seemed to be the only topic they were interested in.

They did not seem ready or willing to discuss other important topics of the day, but Stevie was ready when the moderator asked about America's energy policy. He made the following points:

On President Trump's Energy Policy:

"I think the President has done a great job of reducing our dependence on foreign countries. Now, more than ever before, America is energy-independent, and secure."

On Fracking:

"Fracking has been a huge part of our energy success, according to Forbes Magazine. They've said it has lowered prices and strengthened our security and has brought about less of a dependence on countries in the Middle East."

On Trump's Withdrawal from the International Climate Accords:

"I think the future is nuclear power and it's one of the cleanest forms of energy. But I don't think that pulling out of the climate accords was a bad idea because it took away regulations that were holding us back, and spurred further investment, research, and development."

As the student debate was continuing, it seemed that World War III had broken out among the spectators. One conservative spectator told the Democrats to stay on point. Her Dad was a police officer, and she didn't appreciate the negativity about police. They didn't care. (At least not enough to stop it.)

They simply could not leave the subject of racism behind. And then Andrew said he wanted to talk for a moment about three very important words—Black Lives Matter. "I'm sorry if this is going to offend some people that white males are talking about this...Every single person agrees with that statement. Nobody would disagree and say that black lives don't matter. What people have an issue with is the organization that has co-opted that statement and turned it political. Now, the cofounder of BLM admitted that she and her fellow organizers are trained Marxists. Look at the riots that have occurred in major cities where buildings have been burned down. And consider Portland, where most of the city was taken over for a few weeks. Nobody has an issue with the fact that the lives of black people are just as important as any other people. Every normal person supports the statement. It's the organization that tries to make it political that most Americans do not agree with. BLM and Antifa have destroyed thousands of black owned businesses and have displaced thousands of black residents. They don't care about the stuff they just care about anarchy. Consider David Dorn who was killed by rioters during a BLM riot. They didn't care what the color of his skin was, they didn't care that he served his country, all they cared about was rioting and making a phony political statement."

I had to admire Andrew for his courage. Clearly, Stevie was not the only one on campus who felt the way he did. Unfortunately, Andrew's comments were not well received, and the moderator eventually had to call for order, and move the debate forward.

I knew there were others in the crowd who felt as Stevie and Andrew did, but they kept quiet. There were others, but they were not on SGA or in a fraternity. They choose to keep quiet. How many other students across the country are keeping quiet? Is this the "Silent Majority" we often hear about? If so, we need to do a better job of teaching our children that there are times when we need to speak up, loud and clear.

Perhaps you have heard these powerful words from German Pastor Martin Niemoller:

"First, they came for the socialists, and I did not speak out—because I was not a socialist. Then they came for the trade unionists, and I did not speak out—because I was not a trade unionist. Then they came for the Jews, and I did not speak out—because I was not a Jew. Then they came for me— and there was no one left to speak for me."

And, as Edmund Burke said,

"The only thing necessary for the triumph of evil is for good men to do nothing."

I had heard a lot of troubling things from the liberals who gathered for the debate that day—both from those who were participants and those who had come to observe. But things were about to hit a new low.

A young female spectator sent out a comment in the chat bar bragging that she had obtained an abortion that morning. The tone of her post was jubilant, as if killing her unborn child was something she was proud of.

Someone with a username of "teacher" responded with, "Congrats, exercising your rights."

OUTCAST

The student replied right away. "It was pretty easy, just took a couple pills."

Sick. That's the only word I can think of to describe the way I felt. And it made me feel even sicker to think that the person who congratulated her may have been a Belmont teacher.

As the afternoon wore on, students began insulting their peers, and it was so vicious that one of the moderators said that if the comment section was not respectful, they would turn off the commenting ability. This, of course, was another empty threat and the battles raged on and on, with participants on the chat bar continuing to call the Republicans names.

One student alleged that, "Everyone is racist. It is how we are taught in society. That is how we are racist." Commenting on this, another student said, "It's beneficial to confront your implicit biases and the internalized racism you grew up with in order to work past it." Another self-proclaimed expert chimed in, saying that, "Once you understand sociology, you will understand the implicit bias that lives within all of us."

That came with the response, "Police force exists as a modern-day glorified slavery." This came from "teacher" who may or may not be connected to the university, as we still don't know.

And, speaking about Belmont, one of the students commented that, "To sit here and deny racism on a campus built on slavery is insane." To this, a conservative student asked the question, "If you think Belmont is racist, then why are you paying to be here?"

And thus ended the debate. It was the least productive hour I had ever witnessed, and I was shocked by the laughing, mocking, and hating from the left. This debate had four participants from each side and an audience of 130. At least 100 of those were Democrats. Republicans were truly silent or are there that few of them at a conservative Christian University? One must wonder, but I personally feel the conservatives held themselves back because they had seen the attacks that Stevie had endured, and they were afraid to speak their truth.

9

PROMISES MADE, PROMISES BROKEN

Growing more and more frustrated with the lack of communication for the upcoming Presidential Debate—and especially a lack of clarity as to what his and his VP's roles were, Stevie emailed Belmont's president.

Good morning,

I hope you and your family have stayed safe and healthy during these times. As you may be aware, over the summer there was an incident involving many students attacking me, my family, and many of my friends on one of my posts celebrating being an American on the 4th of July. Sadly, when I am now on campus, I must be with campus security or with friends as threats were made against me and I am unable to be at school alone. I also attend most of my classes on Zoom to avoid any controversy and when I am on campus, I park my car at a nearby friend's garage to not risk anything happening to it...Overall, I feel that I have handled this very diplomatically. In spite of these partnerships, there is still a petition on Change.org that falsely labels me as a racist, calls for my impeachment, and has caused many problems for me.

Unfortunately, this does not look good for the school, SGA, or myself and I truly hope we can take action or have this removed after the debate.

During this time, my Vice President and I have tried to work with the Student Debate Committee in order to stay involved in the debate. Last year, I remember being at a convocation event where you spoke of the Student Body President in 2008, who was able to meet both candidates. This was also told to me by the former dean of students. Unfortunately, it seems that my Vice President and I have been kept in the dark about our roles in the upcoming debate. I feel that my Vice President and I should have an opportunity to welcome the candidates to our school since we are the only two elected students to represent the entire student body and be able to attend the debate. This weekend, I was made aware of the fact that people I knew in the political sphere were being invited to attend the debate, yet my Vice President and I have not heard from anyone making us aware of our roles in meeting and attending the debate.

I know that there is a lot going on and I hope that this has been an oversight or perhaps you were unaware of my Vice President, and I being left out. I would like to clear up the confusion surrounding the upcoming debate and ask about the past promises made to me and my Vice President. Please let me know what my Vice President and I need to do in order to be included in this monumental moment in our Belmont's history. I look forward to hearing from you and seeing you on the day of the debate.

-Stevie Giorno

Within several hours, the president responded with a carefully crafted email. He shrugged off the incident and said there was nothing he could do. All the issues Stevie faced, even the defamation and threats from students under his authority, were supposedly out of his hands. A man making over $2 million a year couldn't get some rowdy, wannabe activists in line to honor a promise that he made.

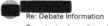

10/14/20

Re: Debate Information

To: stevie.giorno@pop.belmont.edu **Cc:** & 1 more

Details

Dear Stevie,

I hope your classes and SGA operations are going well in these complicated times.

Briefly, I can tell you that the role of students, including how many, if any, will be invited to participate in the Debate process itself is still unknown at this time. In fact, I'm surprised to hear from you that people in the political sphere are being invited to attend the debate. It was only last evening that we were finally able to confirm that our office can invite the Governor and the Mayor to the debate (and that should be held as confidential). The Commission on Presidential Debates routinely holds all of these decisions until the last minute for security reasons and this year, probably to assess the health situations. We're still waiting to learn how many tickets will be available, whether we or someone else (or anybody) will be able to invite other key elected officials, whether a student will be able to greet each of the candidates as occurred in 2008, etc. Once we are able to answer these questions, we will take immediate action.

As for the "Change" petitions, I regret that you have become a target of such a petition. Like much of social media, this organization and its site is a place that thrives on un-truths and mean spiritedness. If you discover a way to remove them let me know--there are several out there attacking me as well.

Dear Stevie,

I hope your classes and SGA operations are going well in these complicated times.

Briefly, I can tell you that the role of students, including how many, if any, will be invited to participate in the Debate process itself is still unknown at this time. In fact, I'm surprised to hear from you that people in the political sphere are being invited to attend the debate. It was only last evening that we were finally able to confirm that our office can invite the Governor and the Mayor to the debate (and that should be held as confidential). The Commission on Presidential Debates routinely holds all of these decisions until the last minute for security reasons and this year, probably to assess the health situations. We're still waiting to learn how many tickets will be available, whether we or someone else (or anybody) will be able to invite other key elected officials, whether a student will be able to greet each of the candidates as occurred in 2008, etc. Once we are able to answer these questions, we will take immediate action.

As for the 'Change' petitions, I regret that you have become a target of such a petition. Like much of social media, this organization and its site is a place that thrives on un-truths and mean spiritedness. If you discover a way to remove them let me know— there are several out there attacking me as well.

The beginning of the Presidential Debate process promised nothing but the bitterness of broken promises. Stevie and his Vice President were still coming to grips with being silenced, wasting half of a year rather than serving their school. They had reached out to every single person they knew to get involved over the entire semester, only to be shut down. Suffice to say, they had no hope for their promised participation in the Presidential Debate. This sentiment was further validated when Stevie was told he could not use his SGA office, especially during the Presidential Debate preparations.

Unfortunately for all those hoping that Stevie's administration would remain quiet and feckless, media outlets do reach out to the SGA president and Vice President. The day after the College Republicans versus Democrats debate, several media outlets reached out to schedule Stevie, asking him to talk about the preparations, the excitement, and the momentum for the debate.

Stevie reached out to his advisor, as that was protocol, and asked him how to handle these requests. His advisor referred him to the communications team, who told him he could not be on campus the day before or the day of the Presidential Debate because everyone supposedly had to be tested for COVID-19, and they had no tests left. She told Stevie he was free to do interviews and to say whatever he wanted to say, but that it could not be done on campus. It was at this point that Stevie realized beyond a shadow of a doubt that Belmont wanted to keep him away from the Presidential Debate. All the "oversights" and "mistakes" were a coordinated effort to keep him away. Stevie had two choices. Right then, he had a captive media audience calling, texting, and emailing him for stories. Because he was SGA President, media outlets were easily able to find his contact information and wanted interviews. Only an idiot would allow an SGA President constantly silenced by Belmont to speak to the press and say whatever he wanted if it was off campus.

My mind raced to understand what was happening. What kind of an administration was this? Who was pulling the strings? Why was Stevie told COVID-19 tests were not available when Stevie knew the facility they were using and had been told to come in any time to take a test?

Stevie respected himself too much to risk losing the Presidential Debate altogether. He wanted President Donald Trump and his opponent, Joe Biden, to be at his university. After all, aren't Republicans the party of freedom of speech?

But hell hath no fury like a mother whose son has been attacked: I am not as forgiving and benevolent as Stevie. He was promised the Debate and I was going to see to it that he got it.

It was 3:25 pm on October 17th, a Sunday, when I phoned Stevie's SGA advisor. I was done with liberals being glorified and Stevie and his Vice President being sidelined. I was done with conservatives suffering for taking the high road. I told him that I completely understood COVID-19 closing the meet and greets, the tours of the school, and all that, but Stevie's not being allowed into the Debate? That was just unacceptable to me.

I reminded the SGA advisor that Stevie won the election unanimously and had the endorsements of both the College Republicans and the College Democrats. This was a student enduring hell from many of the students and the rest of the administration. No one was doing anything. My son was not able to be on campus per campus security yet the Left, who were still a threat to my son, were able to be on campus freely. He agreed it was not fair but out of his control. No, it was totally in his control, and I knew that. I disclosed to him that I possessed a video of campus police escorting Stevie to his classes. My son followed every handbook rule and did everything he was told to. Few classes. No car on campus. Police escort on those rare occasions he had to be at class. No normalcy in his time at Belmont. Isn't it time that the media and public see what is truly going on at a conservative Christian university?

I went on to ask, "Wouldn't that be an interesting tidbit for the media right before the Presidential Debate? Wouldn't this raise many questions regarding why a conservative student body president needed security to walk on campus and would this be a sign of the school's bias against conservatives, especially at a time when the First Presidential Debate was under scrutiny for liberal bias against President Trump?"

I was not after drama. I only wanted what was promised. I will never stand by and allow promises to be broken. This made the advisor change his tune really fast. He promised that Stevie and his Vice President would be hearing from him within hours. I assured him that I would wait until midnight for the good news. Feeling confident we were now both on the same page and

Belmont was honoring the agreement promised at the swearing in ceremony, he and I parted on pleasant terms, and I thanked him for his time. He, too, is a parent after all. I reasoned that he understood where I was coming from.

Later that evening, as promised, an email was sent to Stevie that he and his Vice President would be assisting with the Debate, just as the advisor had promised. Well, they would be ushers. Not exactly what they'd been promised, but it was something. Seeing that Stevie was told they were out of COVID-19 tests, he found it interesting that not only would they be doing interviews with media on campus, but they would also now be at the Debate itself. It seemed, somehow, that more tests had magically appeared. Below is the email Stevie and his Vice President received at 7:50PM on that Sunday night.

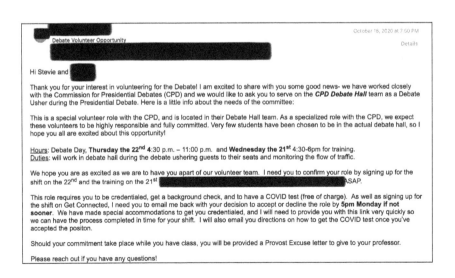

"Thank you for your interest in volunteering for the Debate! I am excited to share with you some good news – we have worked closely with the commission for presidential debates, and we would like to ask you to serve on the CPD debate hall team as a debate usher during the presidential debate, here is a little info about the needs of the committee:

This is a special volunteer role with the CPD, and is located in the Debate Hall team. As a specialized role with the CPD, we expect these volunteers to be highly responsible and fully committed. Very few students have been chosen to be in the actual debate hall, so I hope you all are excited about this opportunity!

Hours: Debate Day, Thursday the 22nd 4:30 p.m. – 11:00 p.m. and Wednesday the 21st 4:30-6pm for training.

Duties: will work in debate hall during the debate ushering guests to their seats and monitoring the flow of traffic.

We hope you are as excited as we are to have you a part of the volunteer team. I need you to confirm your role by signing up for the shift on the 22nd and the training on the 21st ASAP.

This rule requires you to be credentialed, get a background check, and to have a COVID test (free of charge). As well as signing up for the shift on Get Connected. I need you to email me back with your decision to accept or decline the role by 5 PM Monday if not sooner. We have made special accommodations to get you credentialed, and I will need to provide you with this link very quickly so we can have the process completed in time for your shift. I will also email you directions on how to get the COVID test once you've accepted the position.

Should your commitment take place while you have class you will be provided a provost excuse letter to give to your professor.

Please reach out if you have any questions!"

The next day, Monday, October 19th, Stevie, and his Vice President made their way to the health facility set up to act as the COVID-19 testing center for the Debate. There were dozens of classmates and fellow faculty being tested and there was never any mention in the news or even at the school of the health facility running out of tests.

After being cleared of COVID-19, Stevie and his Vice President attended Debate Hall training. During this time, the Commission on Presidential Debates and some Belmont faculty gave a tour to all the students who would be inside the Debate Hall. Interestingly, there were dozens of other students who were given COVID-19 tests and did not have to fight for something that was promised to them.

Coincidentally, many of these students were liberals who were very critical of Stevie's stand against the radical left. In fact, one of the faculty members chaperoning the group was caught by Stevie and his Vice President recording them on his cell phone as they were walking around the Debate Hall. I am not sure what the point of that was to this day.

10

THE PRESIDENTIAL DEBATE

O n the day of the Presidential Debate, Stevie was scheduled for media interviews, so on his way in, he stopped off at his favorite daily fast-food establishment for his breakfast.

He didn't know that one of the girls who was on the Zoom Debate—and a vocal hater of Stevie's—worked at this establishment. He had no idea who she was, other than that she was a barista. On the other hand, she certainly knew who he was.

It seems that the university's College Democrats had a GroupMe chat, in which they fantasized about harming Stevie. One of the members in this chat, a female student named Lindsey had bragged about giving Stevie "gross tea" when he came into the fast-food restaurant where she worked. She joked about facing an attempted murder charge if people knew how often she had done this – apparently it had happened every time Stevie came into the establishment, and he had breakfast there almost every day. The following is a part of one of the group texts:

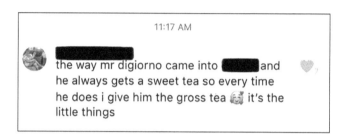

11:17 AM

the way mr digiorno came into ▓▓▓▓ and he always gets a sweet tea so every time he does i give him the gross tea 🧋 it's the little things

Lindsey: "The way 'Mr. DiGiorno' came into the restaurant, and he always gets a sweet tea so every time he does, I give him the gross tea. [hearts emoji] its the little things"

She knew his name but always referred to him as 'Mr. DiGiorno'. Several people liked her comment, which prompted one of Stevie's friends to intervene. Michael, a Democrat friend of Stevie's, also in this group chat, was not going to ignore how terrible her actions were and commented to everyone in the group:

"Ok, I'm sorry y'all, but I need to say this. I really don't appreciate how y'all talk about Stevie. He's a close friend of mine, and people in this group give him way too much shit. Yes, he is a Republican. So what? Just because he is does not make him racist. He just has a different view of how problems should be solved... I stayed quiet while all the stuff over the summer happened because I thought it was a mixture of bad timing and high tension, but seeing people go after a person I consider a friend is something I won't stand for."

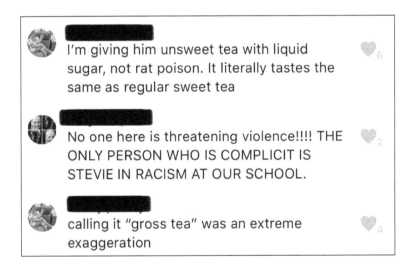

Lindsey quickly backtracked and texted "I'm giving him unsweet tea with liquid sugar, not rat poison. It literally tastes the same as regular sweet tea. Calling it 'gross tea' was an extreme exaggeration.

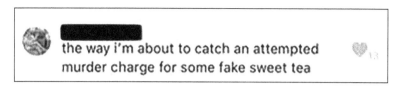

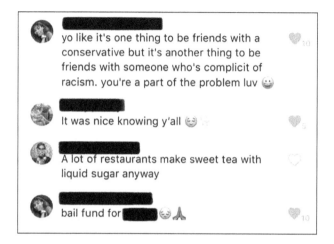

"the way I'm about to catch an attempted murder charge for some fake sweet tea. It was nice knowing y'all."

Other students defended Lindsey's remarks, saying that Michael was the problem for being friends with a racist. One female student, jokingly called for a bail fund to be created for Lindsey.

> **Morgan:** "yo like it's one thing to be friends with a conservative, but it's another thing to be friends with someone who's complicit of racism. you're a part of the problem luv"

She then followed this message with an additional statement of support for Lindsey calling for a "bail fund for Lindsey."

Lindsey then called Stevie a "Chad" and said she had to fight the urge not to physically attack him.

Lindsey: "It's the way that one of the chads is our sga president like, [vomit emoji] … also, it's the way that I saw 'mr. digiorno' at my work this morning and had to fight the urge to throw hands."

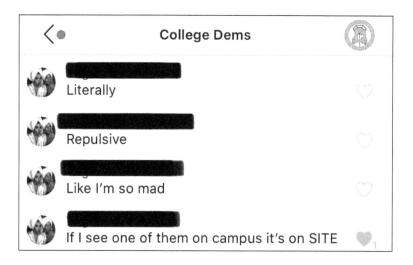

Veronica: "Literally. Repulsive. Like I'm so mad. If I see one of them on campus, it's on SITE." — slang for automatically attacking someone.

Stevie sent this to campus security, and they suggested that he call our local police as the students were not living on campus at the time of these threats. He did as they said but was told that since Lindsey did not live in our town, he would need to call the Nashville Police Department to file a report.

Our family has always been a supporter of law enforcement. In 1995, our family lost a cousin, who was a Chicago police officer. He was killed in the line of duty. We back the Blue. I have always taught my children to respect and honor the police officers that keep us safe. It was also a major reason for Stevie's refusal to support Black Lives Matter.

Stevie called the Nashville Police Department and after waiting for a long period of time due to there being a major shortage of police and first responders in Nashville, he finally got through. Nashville police had offered to meet him in one of their new buildings that was empty at the time due to staffing shortages and said that since he did not have physical injuries, they would not have the resources to investigate a charge of battery. The big city police had also failed us.

Stevie gave all the hateful and threatening texts to the school, but once again, nothing was done. And what punishment awaited these students who had violated basic human decency and practically every rule in the Belmont Student Handbook? Lindsey was accepted into Belmont's Law School even though the school was aware she had committed a crime. Every rule in the handbook on inappropriate behavior was followed by my son. No one at Belmont did a thing. This student full of hate and vengeance was still accepted to Belmont's Law School. How could this school, conservative or not, fail EVERY student so much? When would anyone take any action against her or others in the future? What would happen when the next conservative student body president was attacked as he had been? When would the university finally decide to act?

Despite that crazy day, Stevie was shown on FOX news while at the Presidential Debate and he was honored to have been there. Stevie was still the SGA President and wanted to leave a legacy for the next president to build on. Throughout the summer and into the fall semester, he had routinely met with the Black Students Association, the Asian American Students Association, and the Hispanic Students Association to hear their concerns and come up with solutions so that they would be better represented in student government.

His team worked on a bill that would allow a representative from each of these groups to be a part of Student Government and be able to voice the concerns of their members to the entire SGA. This bill allowed these groups to have liaisons to ensure that their concerns were being heard. Once again, the administration prevented Stevie and SGA from working with students and left him out to dry as he received more and more complaints of inaction on his part. What was truly a shame was that because of the administration attempting to limit SGA and curtail their authority, this bill took much longer to be passed than it should have as Belmont did not want SGA to hold meetings.

Stevie's final goal was to ensure a fair election for his successor. With Belmont still being remote and completely on Zoom, there was a concern about low turnout. However, with all the students that attacked Stevie and SGA, shouldn't that mean there would be a higher turnout of students who actively wanted to participate in their school's election?

It didn't turn out that way. In fact, there was very little turnout. It seemed that all the people who had been sideline quarterbacks were not involved in SGA at all. Why did this happen? Unless these students had just targeted Stevie because of his conservative beliefs, would they continue to be involved in trying to better their university? The answer was no, because these bullies had moved on once they realized that Stevie would not be pushed or coerced into doing anything he thought was wrong. Fortunately, a fellow like-minded conservative, who was supportive of Stevie, won the next election.

11
THE FINAL SEMESTER

Unbeknownst to most of us, at the start of the Spring 2021 semester, some of Stevie's teachers had begun to join in on the drama. Now that he was no longer Student Body President, Stevie wanted to finish classes and get on with his life outside of Belmont.

He became more active in our county party GOP and was working to reform the Young Republicans in Williamson County. Belmont was still encouraging all students to be on Zoom and off-campus and asked teachers to have Zoom be offered when possible. Seeing that Stevie was taking only political science classes at this time, it should have been no problem for him to do them on Zoom.

Besides, for the first few weeks of the semester, Zoom was perfectly acceptable. However, his senior thesis professor began to encourage students to return to the classroom. When few did, his encouragement became a requirement, in direct contradiction to the university guidelines.

Stevie was one of many students who did not understand the change. One of Stevie's classmates emailed the professor and asked for clarification on the decision. That professor responded saying that the class would do better in person and that it would make it easier for him to teach it. He also cc'd a dean in the Political Science program, as well.

The next morning, the dean accidentally replied to both that student and the professor and attacked both the student and Stevie! Stevie had NOTHING to do with this email.

Stevie knew the female student who had asked the question, but he had no prior discussion with her about her email. Why would a dean who pretended to be our friend involve my son who had NOTHING to do with this?

> On Wed, Mar 10, 2021 at 7:29 AM ▉
> Yeah, Stevie and ▉ represent that long line of students who enjoy professional politics but don't bring the same energy to the classroom (e.g. ▉). Sorry you are dealing with this.

The anger I still feel about this is overwhelming. The discrimination and double talk disgusts me to this day, especially when I consider the dean's response: "Yeah, Stevie and [female student] represent that long line of students who enjoy professional politics but don't bring the same energy to the classroom (e.g. male student). Sorry you are dealing with this."

This is the same person who recruited Stevie to Belmont when he was in high school, and who I thought had been supportive of him during the time when he was under siege from the radical left. I could not understand for the life of me how Stevie came up in this email chain to begin with. The student who emailed the professor did not bring Stevie up, nor was he mentioned anywhere else in the email chain. This student who sent the email responded that because it was a hybrid class, she believed that it was optional to participate in person and did not mean to cause an issue. When the dean realized his mistake, he was quick to apologize to her and blamed it on students in another class saying, "Tensions between my students and me are at an all-time high." Despite being aware that Stevie had received a copy of his email, he never mentioned it, nor apologized for his "irresponsible reply" as he would put it. Here is his reply to the female student:

No need to apologize▓▓▓▓▓. I'm the one that needs to apologize. This has been the roughest semester for me in a while, and I am struggling with defining the proper responsibilities that my students should take on in Hybrid settings . Tensions between my students and me-- especially in 1210 settings-- are at all-time high. However, that doesn't excuse my irresponsible reply.

I need to better recognize the contributions that my students are making in real world settings and the difficulties they face in balancing serious public policy responsibilities with academic requirements.

So, for what it's worth, I apologize for my thoughtlessness.

"No need to apologize. I'm the one that needs to apologize. This has been the roughest semester for me in a while, and I am struggling with defining the proper

responsibilities that my students should take on in Hybrid settings. Tensions between my students and me—-especially in 1210 settings—- are at all-time high. However, that doesn't excuse my irresponsible reply.

I need to better recognize the contributions that my students are making in real world settings and the difficulties they face in balancing serious public policy responsibilities with academic requirements.

So, for what it's worth, I apologize for my thoughtlessness."

Because Stevie would need to be back on campus, he followed the advice of campus security and told them when he would be back on campus. They once again advised him to remain off campus to prevent any issues with students still stuck on the fact that he loved America and would not apologize for it. With being so close to graduation and being away from the craziness on university campuses, he was going to follow their advice and remain on Zoom. When he reached out to his professor and told him this, the professor decided to reach out to campus security himself and ask for their assistance. Much to our surprise – although I suppose we shouldn't have been surprised by anything at this point – campus security told the professor that they never said that it was unsafe for Stevie to be on campus!

Somehow, this teacher seemed to have convinced campus security that what had been happening to Stevie for the past six months wasn't that bad, and that the radical left had stopped going after him. In the course of a day, Belmont's message to Stevie went from, "It's unsafe for you to be on campus," to "If you don't show up in person to classes you will fail and not graduate."

The professor referred Stevie to a liberal arts dean for clarification. He called me and was kind but had no idea of anything, much less the severity of all that had been happening on his campus, even though Stevie had provided so many recordings, texts, etc. There was ZERO communication to ensure Stevie's safety, but professors had time to drag him into conversations he was not even a part of! I must wonder, are these professors on campus to teach with conservative values or just there to collect a paycheck and brainwash students along the way?

For Stevie, it was just another road bump along the strange and twisted road toward a college degree. He wanted to graduate and if that meant playing a game with the administration for one more semester and now dealing with harassment from both students and administration, so be it. He continued to park his car at his friend's garage and his friends would pick him up and drive him to and from campus. The discrimination shown to Stevie and the support shown to the radical left was an eye opener! Even at this turning point, Stevie refused to back down. Although masked but recognized and walked to class with friends, Stevie did not back down. I was so proud of him — and terrified at the same time.

Stevie never spoke with these professors again. He expected nothing from a university that hung him out to dry, so why would his professors – even those he had considered to be friends — be any different?

12

GRADUATION DAY

The Bible says, "Let us not become weary in doing good, for at the proper time we will reap a harvest if we do not give up." (Galatians 6:9 NIV)

That's exactly what Stevie did. Our County Republican Party was having its election on April 21st. Stevie was approached by many conservatives who knew what was going on at Belmont. They asked him to run and help lead the county party for the next 2 years. He couldn't say no, because he knew how badly our local Republicans needed new energy and leadership. I was delighted, but not surprised, when Stevie was elected as one of the youngest Republicans to be elected to local office in our county. Stevie knew that the radical left would soon cross over into our conservative county and wanted to take a stand in preparation for what was to come.

As for Stevie's graduation celebration, it was something we as a family talked about often.

Should he not attend?

Should he attend?

What would the reaction be either way? We felt that if he didn't attend, it would be like letting the haters win. In the back of my head was the "it's on site" comment from the young female student and the feeling that it might be best to just skip graduation to avoid any confrontation. Attending could open Stevie to danger. Would the radical students shout at him or boo him? There were so many things that could go wrong. After all, it seemed that everything kept going wrong over the past year.

Stevie didn't agree with me. He wanted to graduate like everyone else — like his older brother before him. He wanted to show that he did not fear his fellow students and that their hatred for him meant nothing. And so, he did.

COVID-19 policies were still being enforced, so the university did not allow for anyone to walk the stage. In addition, everyone was masked, spaced apart in the gym and every student was limited to four guests. The graduates sat on the gym floor and in the stands. Stevie was one of those graduates, placed at the top of the auditorium along with the other Social Science majors. He was surrounded by the haters, the College Democrats, and masked, but they still all knew each other and Stevie sat there without a care in the world.

Eventually, the dean got to the Politics and Public Law graduates and got closer and closer to calling Stevie's name. With every name that was called, the feeling of dread inside of me grew stronger and stronger. Stevie had made jokes for weeks about how he would be the first graduate to be booed at Belmont and had mentally prepared for it, but I had not.

I know that I have never been prouder and more nervous at the same time. As the dean announced his name, Stevie stood up, took off his mandated mask, gave a Trump-style thumbs up and waved to the deans, President, and the haters. Our family applauded as I remember my eyes filling with tears.

He did it! He didn't threaten anyone. He didn't confront anyone. After everything that the left and university officials let go on, Stevie graduated with dignity and self-respect. He had no concerns about his future as he knew he was staying on his path of being a conservative Christian. He had no need to fight. He had won without saying a word.

13

AFTERTHOUGHTS AS THE BATTLE GOES ON

I t's no longer easy for conservative Christian parents to send their children to college. Before sending them out among the wolves, we parents must be sure that our children know who they are and why they think as they do. Otherwise, they risk being compelled by the woke mob. I think of what Jesus said when he sent His disciples out to preach the Gospel: "I am sending you out like sheep among wolves. Therefore, be as shrewd as snakes and as innocent as doves." (Matthew 10:16 NIV)

Today's universities are not what they were when I was in college. They serve to indoctrinate our children into a socialist way of thinking. Even conservative Christian universities honor the terror groups targeting our children and we are helpless unless other parents speak out as I have. We need to rise up and reach out to trustees, donors and call out universities that misrepresent who they really are. Do donors know where their money is going? Universities are not in the business of teaching our students how to think but rather teaching them what to think. Professors will bully our children just as much as the left mob if they are not liberals.

Once happy, well-adjusted teenagers emerge from universities as little Stalins, intent on destroying anyone who disagrees with the narrative set by social media and the mainstream media. As I have walked through all this with my son, I have learned more than I wanted to about bullying, the radical left, haters, universities caving to the left, and the disgrace of administrators not taking threats to their students seriously.

I will never forget the fear, riots, and America's descent into the fires of hell. As the radical left, BLM and Antifa were burning cities to the ground, there was also a call for major cities to "defund the police." Vaccine mandates were becoming commonplace and "vaccine passports" were being forced upon us. The 2nd Amendment was under attack and most of all, pro-life groups were being silenced.

The core values and beliefs of why we fled a blue state were under attack. My son is a perfect example of what happens to those who will not comply. They are left to fend for themselves, despite universities that claim to be conservative and Christian. This was very hard for me to accept, and although Stevie got through everything that was hurled at him, I knew there was a group of people who needed help. They were the ones who didn't know if their conservative faith and morals would be upheld any longer and thought they could be hurt.

After graduation, several young female students slowly shared their stories of intimidation and hostility. I discovered that young conservative women across most campuses are being silenced with no safe place for them to turn. Because of this, I founded a 501c-3 in Tennessee. I named it United Women Foundation. It quickly went from being a statewide organization to a nationwide one.

Our members consist of conservative young ladies from across the country, along with many adult members who are ready to mentor and support young conservative women. Conservatives will not be silenced on our watch. We are grass-roots and invite all conservative women to join us. We meet on Zoom, have various meetings, award scholarships to deserving young ladies and send our members to conservative events. Most of all, we connect conservative women to each other. We give them a voice. It is a place to serve and help conservative women of all ages, backgrounds, and ethnicities. I am proud of what we have achieved in the past few years and of every member we have.

What still inspires me to this day, is that despite the hundreds of negative comments, dozens of conservative students backed Stevie in his Instagram post. I believe that our society is very similar to this. We need one person to light the spark underneath the large group of conservatives that have remained quiet due to fear of the mob attacking them for their love of their country.

Today, the radical mob has infiltrated every aspect of American society. Sports, stores, and universities have all joined the movement to silence conservatives. Ask any conservative college student and you will hear a similar story as Stevie's. It happens every day in all 50 states. It is incumbent upon us as citizens to call out this evil when we see it. We can no longer comply with BLM and other radical left groups pushing their agendas down our children's throats. We can no longer be scared to speak out for fear of reprisal or attack. None of the evil in America is going to change and there will be more stories, like Stevie's, unless you and I decide enough is enough. So, what does that look like for you and me? Boycotts. Affecting the bottom line has the potential to turn this ship around. While it may be bleak now, if we are unable to change course, I foresee a terrible evil affecting the future generations of America and there will be no one to blame except you and I for letting it happen.